Arthur N Howard

Life's Real Romance

A Picture from Life from 1838 to 1883

Arthur N Howard

Life's Real Romance
A Picture from Life from 1838 to 1883

ISBN/EAN: 9783337067311

Printed in Europe, USA, Canada, Australia, Japan

Cover: Foto ©ninafisch / pixelio.de

More available books at **www.hansebooks.com**

LIFE'S

REAL ROMANCE.

A PICTURE FROM LIFE

FROM

1886 TO 1883.

PUBLISHER'S PREFACE.

This book is exactly what it is named. There is no fiction in it except the names, which I have changed at the writers request. As most of the characters in it are living. I give it to the public in the same condition in which it was written, in a journal of every day life. All of this first volume was written by a relative of mine and his son, excepting a few incidents in the parts on England and Canada, and the fragmentary verses and criticisms which are by myself.   R. A. N. H.

CHAPTER I.

Incidents in the life of Jonathan E. Howard, as recorded by his son, Arthur N. Howard from manuscript and letters given him by his father. J. E. Howard was born in 1819. "When 19 years of age I was sent to my oldest brother Timothy Howard an insurance agent in the town of Waterford, but preferring mechanics to a comercial life, I returned to Cork my native city. After 12 months residence with my brother, my father applied to a friend of his, an architect in Belfast to have me indentured to him. But he asked the sum of £500 premium and £150 a year for board and clothing which was not accepted as my father preferred to have me nearer home and ultimately articled me to Mr. John Duncan, who was much indebted to some cousins of mine, who were engaged in the lumber business, whereby I was taken without premium, and boarded at home. Mr. Duncan was architect to the Eccleciastical commissioners also to the harbor board of the the city of Cork. The indenture was made out as follows: This indenture witnesseth that Jonathan E. Howard, son of Timothy Howard of the City of Cork, architect, doth put himself apprentice unto John Duncan of the city of Cork, architect and master builder, to learn his art with him, after the manner of an apprentice from the seventeenth of March, 1836, unto the full end and term of seven years, from thence next following to be fully completed and ended, from which term the said apprentice his said master faithfully shall serve, his secrets keep, his lawful commands everywhere gladly do. He shall do not damage to his said master, nor see it done by others, but that to his power shall or forthwith give warning to his said master of the same. He shall not waste the goods of his said master, nor give, nor lend them unlawfully to any, he shall not commit fornication, nor contract matrimony within the said term, hurt to his master he shall not do, cause or procure to be done, by others, he shall not play at cards, dice, table, or any other unlawful games whereby his said master may have loss with his own or other goods during the said term. Without license of his master he shall neither buy, nor sell, he shall not haunt or use taverns, ale-houses, nor play-houses, nor absent himself from his said masters service, day nor night unlawfully, but in all things as an honest, faithful apprentice, he shall behave himself to his said master during the said term of seven years. And said John Duncan, his said apprentice in the same art which he useth, by the best way and means that he can, shall teach and instruct, or cause to be taught and instructed, with the correction finding unto his said apprentice for the last two years of said term, according to the custom of the, and for the preformance of, all and every, the said contracts and agreements, either of said parties bindeth themselves to the other by these presents. In witness whereof, the said parties above named to these indentures, have interchangeably put their hands and seals.

The first three years was chiefly in the office, at drawing and calculations, and in the workshops at modelling etc., during which apprenticeship I had a very happy time in being engaged in things more congenial to my tastes than merchantile life. Not only then engaged at the office work but also much travelling about to visit works during their execution, comprising of repairs to some churches and the building of free churches to the south of Cork City besides similar works to private residences. Also the superintending of the building of work-houses in Cork, Kilmallock, Dungarven and elsewhere. Also quays and other waterworks at Cork and Queenstown, on some of which were employed as many as four hundred men, including mechanics and laborers the former averaging three shillings per day, the latter ten pence in country places, and in cities somewhat higher, which is a great contrast to the present rates. We assisted Mr. James Arton, Architect of the board of public works, of Dublin, in taking soundings along the River Lee, when the tide was out, for the line of the reclaiming wall. As there was a broad tract of the shallow bed of the river exposed when the tide was out, over which a railroad was to run. Which tract of land has since been reclaimed by building a long, high, retaining wall, (called the Navigation wall) to keep the deeper channel free from mud, and also to keep the water from the shallow bed that was reclaimed, which has since been made a park and pleasure ground. We only superintended the building of the navigation wall and the soundings for the line of railway. We had to make wooden sleighs to hold two persons each drawn by men with ropes over the mud, six to each, without their trowsers. This was how the soundings were taken for hard bottom. About this time railways were commenced in Ireland and the route of the Cork & Passage railway was laid out.

While engaged superintending the repairs of Columbine quay, at Queenstown, a very severe storm arose one night, and washed some fishermen and their boats ashore, who were returning heavily laden with fish. chiefly herrings, but the beach being shallow, most of the men were saved. It was quite a scene next morning to see the men, women and children, out in the water, trying to gather the fish. On the south side of this harbor, at a place called Sleiv Rue, Red Mountains, lived a Mr. Gustave Dorrington for whom Mr. Duncan designed a large house and on one occasion, when I went down to see how the work was going on, I saw a large number of horses capering on the highlands near the shore, and was told of a curious occurance regarding an English lady passenger on board a steamer, who was under the impression that some of the Irish were quite wild. When coming near the shore she was shown some of these horse, frisking on the Highland as a specimen of the wild Irish, whether the story is true or not I cannot say, but I was reminded of it by an after occurrence when in the the county of Essex in England, I was actually asked by e, young man by no means devoid of ordinary intelligence, whether it was really true, that some of the Irish were wild. I of course undeceived him.

During the time of my apprentiship I had frequent opportunities when traveling to and from works, of seeing many places of interest. For instance Barry's Court, near Middleton, County of Cork, which is interesting in having a very fine heavy old fashioned dark Irish roof of which there are not many examples. The Abby and Monastery of Kilmallock, is over six hundred years old. Most of the masonry is in excellent condition, the angles of the tower being very accurate and upright, and the tooling on the stone work very apperent, after such a lapse of sime. The tomb of the White Knight and others were in very good order. In the Monastety was a fire-place, the arch of which was perfectly flat and in a perfect condition, which struck me as a remarkable feature of good workmanship, for the age in which it was was built. Not many miles from there on the road to Limeric is a small lake called Lough Zurr, in which is an island, having a small church with a stone roof, over nine hundred years old, and in a tolerable state of preservation. Those sort of roofs, are semi-circular or arched shaped inside, and sloping and pointed like an ordinary roof outside. In this locality are some of the old Palistine and Huguenot refugee families with their long strips of farms, which look conspicious amongst the irregular ones. Running from Tipperary through Limeric, is the celebrated golden vein of land, so called from its fertility being a deep dark loam.

While superintending the building of a work house in Limeric, I had frequent opportunities to take rambles and journeys to various parts or the country. On holidays, which were frequent among catholic workmen, and sometimes on business. When going to Clogheen on business, I saw Mitchelstown and Shanbally castle. The latter, the seat of Lord Lismore, the former, the seat of the Earl ot Mitchelstown. In this castle the dining is ninety feet long, forty feet wide and thirty feet high. It is a much plainer and heavier structure than Shanbally Castle, which is a much handsomer, and more superbly executed piece of architecture, costing ninety-five thousand pounds and was not then entirely finished. While I was taking a sketch of the castle, a servant man came and told me that his lordship said I might see the interior of the castle which I could only do hurridly as I was on my to the celebrated Mitchelstown caves nearly three quarters of a mile underground. They are of limestone formation, with a considerable amount of ctalactites hanging from the roof. I also saw the mansion of Ogrady, called Kilballyowen, which has a very fine park in which were several very handsome, spotted deer they appeared perfectly tame. When some of them were crossing a sunken fence it was perfectly beautiful to see the ease with which they bounded across it. While in this part of the country, I took several very pleasant excursions to a mountain, a few miles off, and to old ruins. While going up the Shinnon, to Killaloe slate-works, I saw some of the effects of the great famine and riots, that occurred at Limeric. Mobs were breaking open bakeries and flour stores in various parts of the city, notwithstanding the efforts of the police and soldiers to check them. On one occasion, I saw a mob pulling sacks of flour out of a ship on to the quay and breaking them open. While doing so they were suddenly suprised by a troop of soldiers who dashed down a street close by, and the foremost trooper threw his lance into the middle of the crowd; and it struck in a bag of flour without hurting any one, but it had the effect of frightening them off, which was all the soldiers wanted. And they made very few arrests, out of pity to the people. With the finishing of this work house my time was up with Mr. Duncan, and I returned home.

CHAPTER II.

I remained at home a few months: while there my cousins, the Derwents, who were in the timber business, wanted me to set up in Cork, as Mr. D. was about to retire, having made a considerable amount of money. But I had conceived a desire about this time of going to London to see public works and buildings of a superior kind, and so declined their kind offer. In the fall of 1840 I started for London, taking steamer from Waterford. We encountered a severe gale off the Saltee Islands, and though it was my first trip to sea I was not at all sick. Next morning we got near Bristol; I was interested at the sight of a great bar chain high up in the air across the river from hill-side to hill-side, which was the commencement of preparations for a suspension bridge. I was not long in England before I was struck with the contrast between it and Ireland from the scenery on my way from Bristol to London. It was not only the different character of the country (more flat and rolling and not so hilly as Ireland) but there was a greater air of comfort and neatness about all the places we saw on our way. But on arriving at the great metropolis my feelings of surprise were still greater on beholding the vast multitude of people and vehicles moving about in all directions, and the almost endless houses and streets. As my place of abode was to be near the east end of London, close to London Bridge, I had a long journey by omnibus through crowded streets. I felt almost as if I would never get to the end of the journey. I had a letter to Mr. Iite, the architect of the Royal Exchange, but as he had no vacancy just then he gave me an introduction to Messrs. Starling and Morton, the church and work-house architects, which kind of work I was more used to. They had no vacancy either, but promised me one in a few weeks. In the meantime I went sight seeing.

I went one morning early before breakfast to the top of St. Paul's, into the ball underneath the cross at the top of the cupola; it is said to be something over three hundred and seventy feet high, and the ball is twelve feet in diameter, made of sheet copper gilded on the outside, as is also the cross. They are supported by several strong bars of metal about three or four inches thick. The object of going up early was to get a good view of the city before the smoke of the numberless houses and factories obscured the atmosphere, and certainly it was a grand view. Horses drawing omnibuses in the streets reminded one of the industrious fleas that an ingenious individual harnessed to a coach; and though St. Paul's is on a tolerable rise of ground, the whole city and country around appeared somewhat like a great basin; at this time the city was nine miles wide and fifteen long. Underneath are numerous monuments of notable persons, and over the center is the great whispering gallery—circular. When a person drops a hankerchief at one side it bounds to a person at the other side as if a sack of grain had fallen. On going into one of the clock towers in the front it happened to strike for the quarter, and the noise was so sudden and close that it made one deaf for some minutes after. There is also a vast library in the church. A short time after this the great fire of the Tower of London took place. It happened just at the time the great moat was empty of water. It was not the tower itself but the great armory adjoining it, and the conflagration was irresistible on account of the want of water. The several floors of the armory were loaded with stands of arms, all of which I had fortunately seen some days before the fire took place. It was a terrible loss that could not be repaired, as many of the arms were relics of ancient victories. I went a few days after to see the ruins, and not only the small arms were melted and distorted but even cannon were rendered useless. The center tower was uninjured so that Queen Elizabeth's or the horse armory escaped damage. In the chambers where prisoners of former days were confined, inscriptions may be seen cut in the wall by them. Another place of great interest to spend the day is the British Museum at which it would at least take a week to get acquainted with it. The library is immense. The collections of stuffed birds and animals, fossils, skeletons of antediluvian and other animals are extremely interesting. There is a skeleton of a great mammoth found in Labrador, under which the skeleton of an elephant stands crossways. The massive legs are perfectly surprising; the fore legs differ from the elephant's in having claws instead of toes and they bend upwards like a human arm. It has no probosis like the elephant, and the tusks are longer and more slender, bending horziontally sideways. It is supposed to enable it to make its way through the heavy cane brake and reeds of the age it lived in. It seems to have had the habit of sitting on its hind quarters and scratching up roots on which it fed with its fore claws and passing them up to its mouth, because the circular bend of the tusks would prevent them from putting their mouths to the ground. The fossiliferous remains of other antediluvian animals such as flying lizards and other extraordinary reptiles are exceedingly interesting as showing the early date of the world. There were also splendid collections of minerals. Westminster Abbey like St. Paul's is a splendid monument of architectural skill, but being a Gothic edifice takes our thoughts back to a different age and people from that of St. Paul's which is a common style of architecture. The former has been more honored with the monuments of kings and great men of which there are some splendid specimens, such as Henry the Seventh's chapel. Here may be seen the coronation chair and the stone brought from Scotland of which it is traditionally said that no king will ever reign in Scotland till it is returned to their throne again. At the north side of Charing Cross is the national gallery, which contains the national collection of paintings of all masters both ancient and modern. One day would only allow a cursory glance through them. A lover of fine arts could spend more than an hour in gazing on one of them. At the head of Regent street is the Polytechnic Institution where scientific lectures are given, and models of various kinds of works of art, curious and ingenious inventions are deposited for exhibition. There is a diving bell suspended in water, into which many people go for the novelty of it. Farther on at the north side of Regent's Park is to be seen the celebrated zoological gardens where may be seen many of the most remarkable birds, animals and reptiles of the world. They are too numerous to give a short description of and even to take a hurried glance at the whole of them would take a full day. There are very nice refreshment places where tea, coffee, cakes and sweetmeats can be had at reasonable prices by those who wish to spend a very pleasant and interesting day in the gardens. The young people are mostly entertained with mischievous monkeys, talkative parrots and rides on elephants. Grown people find attraction in the crocodiles, snakes and other reptiles, orang-outangs, hippotamus and elephants and their young. Their neighbors the rhinocerous even in their captive state show their great antipathy to the elephent by putting their heads over the fences and trying to fight with them. The hippopotamus delights in rolling about in the water and occasionally opens his enormous jaws when the people throw him something to induce him to do so. The numerous bears afford considerable entertainment, chiefly the cinnamon, white and grizzly. In going on to the sloth and other minor species a sort of relationship is easily perceived between them and the bears. At four o'clock the feeding of carnivorous animals becomes a great attraction to see them bounding over each other and howling for their food. The reptile house is also a considerable attraction; but it is rather a melancholy sight to see the poor rabbits, goats and fowls shivering with terror when the reptiles fix their glittering eyes on them before darting upon their prey. The seals are remarkably interesting from their docile and affectionate ways.

The gardens are laid out with considerable taste, winding walks with flowers and evergreens. Also an imitation of fair Rosamond's bower, where some people amuse themselves trying to find their way through the labyrinth. In Regent's Park, near to Regent street, are the beautiful botanical gardens where almost endless varieties of flowers and plants may be seen in various stages of perfection. The Kew gardens are also very attractive with their numerous green-houses and conservatories and the interesting museum of curiosities from the South Sea Islands and other places. Also the ponds with the celebrated plants called Victoria Regina spreading themselves upon the surface. At the head of Regent street is also the Diorama, an immense circular picture of London and its surroundings as taken from the top of St. Paul's. It is seen from an elevated position in the center representing the cupola of St. Paul's and is very interesting to those who would not like to make the ascent of the other. Madame Tousseau's exhibition of wax work figures is also well worth seeing: here may be seen representations of all ranks of society, such as crowned heads, statesmen, warriors, men of learning and criminals, all in juxtaposition forming remarkable contrasts in their various costumes of the past and present age. London also at that time contained many remarkable contrasts in buildings. The great overhanging wooden edifices of former ages in older streets contrasting very much with the splendid brick and stone architecture of the present time. Some of the old ruins with their internal and projecting galleries above and around the square had much of comfort and convenience in them. But city ground has risen so much in value that many of those old relics are fast giving place to modern improvements, wider streets, splendid squares and parks, adding greatly to the health of that enormous city. Considering its former narrow streets with houses projected above, almost shutting out the daylight; gargoyles or projecting water-spouts from the roof dropping water on the people's heads, and only surface drainage retaining much filth and dirt and crowded tenements, it is no wonder that there should have been a plague in the earlier days of London. The underground sights are a wonder in themselve; the enormous water-pipe and gas-pipe arrangements adding greatly to the health and comfort of the city. Much of this can be seen when the workmen enter boats to perform repairs in the main sewers. In addition to this, in eighteen hundred and sixty, the underground railway was in course of construction to relieve the enormous traffic on the streets above. Life on the Thames even then was as great a contrast to the former ages as that on land. The enormous amount and variety of water craft, crowded steamers with their living freights, heavy barges with goods, and numberless varieties of smaller crafts down to the tiny wherry propelled by sails and oars crowded the surface of the river almost as much as people and vehicles on the streets.

And I often think it is most wonderful, to think how few accidents there are in proportion to the vast amount of traffic going on. I have often had to wait over fifteen minutes—unless I made a dash between or under horses—to cross the street, which I was often obliged to do as well as others. Though the London Bridge of the present day is a splendid contrast to the old one with its crowded houses on each side, the traffic while I was there was so dense it was quite a tedious matter for either people or vehicles to cross over faster than at a moderate walk. At the west end the streets are not so crowded, and out-door sights are more easy. The horse guards at the entrance of Green Park are splendid specimens of humanity, every man over six feet high clad in helmet and cuirass, sitting on large heavy horses. One need not wonder on beholding them that they were able to accomplish what they did at Waterloo. The Queen's Palace in the park is a contrast to the old St. James, where the state ceremonies are held, by an order from the Lord Chamberlain. After a suitable reference or introduction one can get to see the palace. It was very amusing on one occasion, when standing near the staircase, to see the Queen pass down to lunch; the Queen small and dignified and the great big Duchess of Sutherland following after. Farther down the river is Chelsea Hospital, the last home of old pensioned soldiers, which forms an attraction to the lovers of military life—where those who prefer hearing tales of military heroism from the lips of the disabled participants can do so. Farther down is the Greenwich Hospital, the home of the naval pensioners, where the poor old fellows are just as proud to relate their anecdotes. The hospital is a very fine commodious building facing the river on the side of a hill, with large squares for walking about in fine weather and long open galleries for wet weather. They have a good view of their native element, with ships, steamers and boats plying up and down the river. It is quite an interesting sight to see them sitting down to long rows of tables to their meals apparently very happy. Farther up the river are the Greenwich and Deptford dockyards, where enormous ships are built under equally enormous roofs with top lights in them. In numerous sheds are stowed away classified parts of a ship ready to be put together on the shortest notice in case of war or any other emergency. The government have also very fine dockyards at Chatham and Sheerness, farther down the river, of which I took some sketches from the hill-side. The fortifications partly consist of deep and broad excavations, called the lines of Chatam, and a sight worth seeing. The great docks in the neighborhood of London for commercial shipping are a grand sight, not only on account of their great magnitude but as giving the vast idea of the great amount of London's trade and commerce by sea, the chief of which are the London, the East and West India and the commercial docks. Near here is the great Thames Tunnel made considerably below London Bridge, as a bridge would be extremely inconvenient to shipping there. It was not open all the way through when I went to see it. They were working from both sides of the river towards the middle, and four days after I had been in it the water burst in the second time since it was begun. The apertures in the bed of the river were filled by dropping in bags of sand. The water was then pumped out and work resumed. The tunnel is a double one formed by brick and cement, with archways communicating with each side. It was completed long before I left, and has been lit with gas. Numerous stalls with venders of fancy articles for sale occupy the middle spaces, blowers of glass toys in some fruit stalls and music going on in others; while enormous shipping

2

from foreign lands float past over this underground traffic. The engineer
of this tunnel is the son of Mr. Brunell, who designed the Great Eastern.
The first sight of her amongst other ships reminded me of an elephant
amongst other animals.

CHAPTER III.

I Spent about two months sight seeing till I got an occupation, the
first of which was surveying and mapping of building property about London for an architect, a Mr. Voley near London bridge, afterwards street-
surveying in the south of London for a Mr. Johnson, engineer at Charing
Cross, to make a map of premises, etc., for a water pipe company, also
helping him with others for extensions and improvement of Buckingham
Palace It had been the residence of the Duke of Buckingham formerly,
but was extended and enlarged as a private city residence of the Queen.
After this I got employment with Hart & Morton, the great church archi-
thects and was for some weeks engaged in their office, making working
drawings for a new church, and the repairs of an old one at Dover which
I was to go down and superintend the execution of. When it was nearly
ready for commencement, I was sent to the Countess of Ecclestone, an
old maid who was the principal subscriber to the works. She had a peculiar objection to unmarried persons and though Mr. Morton warned me
not to let her know I was unmarried, she asked me so pointedly that I
not avoid telling her, but foolishly forgot to tell her that I was engaged
and hoped to be married soon. The fact was I was taken by surprise,
not altogether thinking that Mr. Morton's warning was really in earnest
but rather a joke as he was a very pleasant person. It was a great disappointment to me when she said she would not have an unmarried person
to superintend her works as it would have been a lucrative and pleasing
occupation.

Dover, being the great channel of communication between France
and England, some months before this in the spring of 1841, I became acquainted with a young lady from Cork, named Miss Goldsmith whose
brother was a medical man in London to whom she came to keep house.
She had been acquainted with one of my sisters, and my father wrote to me
saying that he wished me to become acquainted with them as her brother
might introduce me to some of his acquaintances who might be of service
to me in my profession, and after my previous disappointment, decided to
study the medical profession which I did for some years, taking a very
great interest it but finally for various reasons gave up. Shortly after I
received the superintending of some alterations and repairs of the premises
of a large leather carrying firm, Mr. C. Jenkins & Sons after which the
London & Brighton Railway Company required some extension from their
terminus near London bridge. It nececessitated the removal of Queen
Elizabeth's Grammar School. My former friend Mr. Foley, architect to
the governors of the School, gave me the superintendency of the work.
When this was finished I got an engagement to go and survey some wood-
land on Lord Darnley's estate near Gravesend in Kent.

I was greatly surprised one day, by a large flock of pheasants rising
up in the air in front of me and only going a short distance aside. The

wood-ranger told me that his Lordship was a minor, and that there was no
shooting done on the place which was the cause of the pheasants being
so re markably tame.

Passing by the premises one day, I caught sight of a curius old fashioned coach. The coach and wheels were gilded all over. I was informed
that it was a coach of Mary, Queen of Scots and then I remembered that
the Darnley family were connected with her.

While in Kent I saw many places of interest and some beautiful scenery.

There is a canal running from Gravesend to Chatham, running a considerable way under the cliffs. While here I went to Canterbury, being
curious to see the place where Thomas A. Becket was murdered.

On returning to London I got an engagement from Meesrs Harting &
Morton to superintend the repairs of a church in Essex, at Corringham.
While doing so I had an attack of fever and ague, as did also many of the
working men. Several of the men died on account of their drinking habits. I returned to London as soon as I was well enough and put myself
under the care of Dr. Goldsmith. While there, I was nearly poisoned by
a young lady who was under the Doctor's care because I, at the request of
the Doctor, had prevented her from having interviews with a gentleman
visitor whom the Doctor did not approve of, but fortunately the Doctor
arrived in time to give me antidotes which checked the effect of the tartar
emetic that had been given me, but as I was still in delicate health I had
to refuse an offer from Messrs Harting & Morton and go to Ireland for a
change of air. When after a few months I had recovered, I got an engagement with Sir John McNeill, the engineer of Dundalk & Enniskulan
Railway.

CHAPTER IV.

When the railway was finished I went to the South to see my
relatives at the city of Cork, and to spend some time visiting friends and
acquaintances. After this I went to Dublin. On my way there, I was
surprised to meet an old college chum with whom I had become occuainted
while studying engineering at King's College, London. He was superintending a large number of men digging drains in a bog and burning the
surface when dry, then spreading the clay from the bottom of the drains
on the surface. Some of the drains were twelve feet deep. He set potatoes in the ground and when the people saw the good yield, he readily
sold the land at a profit and bought more elsewhere to do the same.

There was some unusual delay at Cashel which gave me an opportunity to go out and take a scetch of some old ruins on the great rock by the
town. While touching up my scetches at the hotel, I observed a tall gentleman looking over my work. We got into conversation and I found
that he was an American gentleman from Philadelphia. I asked him if he
ever went to New York and he replied : O yes quite frequently. I then
told him I had a cousin there, named James Howard. What ! he said
with some surprise, he is one of my particular friends. I always stop at
his place when I go to New York. He gave me his card with an invita-
taon to go and see him if I ever came to America. He was traveling
with his son and daughter for their health. His name was J. Jackson,

Senator.   I found out afterwards that he visited my father at Cork.

Shortly after my arrival at Dublin, I got a contract for building orna-mental houses for the giraffe, elephant, and camel, in the Zoologicl Gar-dens, Phœnix Park.   While here I had several building contracts.   The great potatoe famine occured about this time and I helped to make some of the soup-houses for the relief of the poor in Dublin.   It was very dis-tressing to see the poor wornout creatures from the country sit down on the door-steps, some of whom were never able to rise again, yet I have known flour merchants who have had quantities of their flour damaged by long holding over on anticipation of exorbitant prices which they never got, as the Americans sent considerable quantities of provisions for the re-lief of the poor.   The Government, and also various denominations but especially the Society of friends.

While finishing the last named works, I was requested by a barrister and his nephew, a clergyman in Bath named Rev. I. Leckie, to make a deviation survey for part of a line of railway between Dundalk and Ennis-kulen to avoid going through their property, but it was necessary to see Mr. Leckie, and as I was anxious to see my friends in London, I went to Bath in company with a friend of mine, an architect of Dublin who wished to join me in the survey.   On seeing Mr. Leckie, we found that the great-er portion of the work would have to be paid by a Post Obit Bond, and for this reason did not take it.

Soon after my return, Smith O'Brien's rebellion broke out.   After settling whatever business I had, I decided to return to London, although several engagements were offered to me.   Shortly after leaving Dublin, I met a steamer from Liverpool with some cavalry and artillery to quell the the rebellion.   Most of the passengers were going over to England to pick hops in Kent.

CHAPTER V.

Some time after my arrival, I got the superintendency of a new church at Crompton for a Mr. Gurney, editor of the *Builder's Newspaper*.   When that was finished I had to go to York to make a svrvey of some property there for a Mr. Kothingham.   York City has antiquated appearance, hav-ing a great portion of the old circular wall still surrounding it, very high, and broad enough for a span of horses and coach to go round on.   There is a grand old cathedral in excellent condition, and an ancient castle used as a court house and town hall.

On my return to London I went to Searborough, on the north-east coast of England, called the queen of watering places, because it so much resembles the Bay of Naples, having a broad, circular beach, sheltered by high, sloping hills.

From Searborough I went to Peterborough to see the Cathedral there, which is small but very handsome, and then went on to Lincoln which has a grander cathedral than that of Peterborough.   To the north of the town, across the main road are two archways, and a portion of the old city wall that was built by the Romans.   The gateways are said to be one of the best specimens of Roman workmanship over ground in England.   There are still some large stones in the roadway, said to be the remains of the ancient Roman road. Saw Ely Cathedral on my way from Lincoln. The town is a very small one and the bishop, although a bachelor and receiving a large income, never contributed a shilling to the improvement of the cathedr al which was undergoing repairs. I went to Cambridge and saw the University. Even its kitchen is quite a sight with its large fireplace and superb cooking arrangements on a large scale.

Not long after this I had to attend the assizes in the transfer of some railway shares by my friend Mr. Rothingham. When it was over we went northwards to his father's estate, called Kingthorpe, near Pickering. It was then let to a wealthy captain in the army. Old Colonel Rothingham being a widower he resided in London with his son. While rambling around Kingthorpe I came across a band of gypsies encamped in the woods. They were the first Gypsies I ever saw and were very numerous but not prepossessing in my opinion. A few days after, we returned to York a nd spent some time there on Mr. Rothingham's estate and then returned to London late in the autumn of 1851.

A short time after this I got married to Miss Goldsmith and moved to Adam's Street Adelphi, near Charing Cross. While there, I became surveyor to the West London Building Society.

CHAPTER VI.

In the following summer, the governors of Queen Elizabeth's grammar school, decided to rebuild it in another part of the parish. I got the superintending of the erection of it. When the drawings were all finished, and the contract given out, I had another journey northwards to Leeds to select building stone for the work from the Hare Hill quarries of which there were three, I choose the middlestone as being of medium quality and good color. One was too hard and brittle and of a poor color, the other was too soft and too dark. I brought specimens with me to compare with what might be brought to the works in case of imposition. The design consisted of a classical and grammar school, three class rooms, two masters' houses, a large board room, a library, covered cloisters for play grounds in wet weather, a handsome tower and cupola one hundred and ten feet high and a handsomely grained open porch approached by a large flight of stone steps. The board room floor was composed of inlaid Mosaic flooring. The whole was heated by hot air furnaces under ground. It was in the Gothic style of the Elizabethian period with a beautifully carved, full sized statue of Queen Elizabeth, in a handsome niche over the porch. The cost of building it was twenty-eight thousand pounds. Besides this I had a considerable amount of work to do to houses in the parish which constituted the support of the school. There were about eighty of them. The work altogether cost somewhat over forty thousands pounds. A short time after that I had finished this engagement, I was attacked by the Asiatic cholera one night, but having received proper remedies from my wife till the doctor arrived I recovered in about a week. The cholera was very prevalent in London at this time. Sometime previous to this the great Iron Duke's death occurred. We had a large party of friends at our house, to view it passing, from the front windows and the top of the house; it was grand and imposing, and not to be easily forgotton by those that saw it.

As my father has ommitted a few incidents in the last few years, I shall mention them as follows: From 1858 to 1860, he earned very little money at his profession. Whether this was caused through his want of energy or dull times is not for me to decide; the reader can judge for himself on reading the sequel. Also that he spent a considerable amount of money and valable time in learning photography with Mr. Rothingham Jr. And also opened a book store, but devoted more time to studying scientific books, than to the business, and in consequence it was a failure. It is, however, quite probable that his want of energy and application in following his profession, and the glowing accounts they had read of America, induced my mother to give her consent to leave her numerous' friends, and generous and devoted brother, in 1860. "In the beginning of 1857, a cousin of my wife, Lieutenant Sanford, asked me to go with him to India, as there were fine prospects for a civil engineer in that country. I had also an offer from an English engineer, which I fortunately did not accept as the Indian mutiny broke out a short time after, and poor Sanford was cruelly massacred while going down the river with a remnant of his company, in a few boats. He was induced to come ashore by Nana Sahib, who told them that if they would deliver their arms and ammunition and surrender, they would only be treated as prisoners of war. There being no alternative, as the banks were lined with rebel troops and cannon, he did so, upon which Nana ordered them all to be shot. Sanford, who hid a revolver in an inside pocket, asked to be brought before Nana, as he wished to speak to him. When brought to the line of guards that surrounded Nana, and could go no further, he shot six of them down, and presented the revolver the last time at Nana himself, but the cap missed and he was seized by the order of Nana and condemned to be sacrificed. His nose and ears were cut off and he was left under a scorching sun all day. Afterward a troop of horsemen were made to ride past him and each one had a cut at him with their swords. His father, on reading an account of it, was so overcome that he fell fainting from his chair, and died a short time after. His wife received a pension, and his two sons— Frank and Henry—obtained commissions in the army. In the year 1858 I received instructions from Mr. Nottingham to advertise and sell his property in Sardinia, consisting of a large estate of eighteen thousand acres, on which was an olive, a mulberry and vine plantation, a very substantial house built of stone, with outoffices and a large collection of books, with stock and implements, which I sold for him for £3,500. It was eleven miles from a seaport, and there was a large tract of swampy land between it and there which generated fever and ague, of which his brother died, for which reason his father wished him to part with it. In 1859 I made several designs for villa residences, costing on an average £1,100, which were afterward sold for £1,400 each. About this time Richard Goldsmith, my brother-in-law in Canada, gave me a lot of land containing one hundred acres, situated seven miles from a village called Aston, which I accepted and decided to emigrate to America. After selling our furniture and bidding our friends adieu, we took train for Liverpool and embarked on board the steamship Bohemia, on which I kept a journal during the voyage.

CHAPTER VII.

Embarked on board the board the Bohemia from Liverpool to Quebec on the 13th day of August, 1860. Capt. G. hauled out of dock at 10:30 a. m. Stood to for the mail and late passengers; got under way and fired signal gun; wind blowing very strong, rather against us and rough, the steamer pitching and rolling; people gradually went below and many were sick, including myself and baby, but not Sarah or Tom; had an extremely rough night passing the Isle of Man: many very sick; saw the coast of Scotland early next morning in the distance; when entering Movile Bay, anchored near the mouth of Loch Foyle to wait for the Londonderry and Glasgow mail and passengers; several went ashore to Movile and Londonderry: Movile is a small watering place, and many nice residences are along the side of the Bay, also some fine old abbey ruins and a revolving light house on the headland to the left going out, which is the last we saw of the British Isles that night or since; saw some sea gulls on the second and third day; wind nearly against us every day, and the ship pitched and rolled very much; there are many showers of rain and heavy mists, some days very fine in the forenoon and tolerably calm; others with strong breeze and sails set to keep the ship steady; people on deck every day, some fine afternoons in considerable numbers; passed a schooner on Sunday morning about four miles off to the southward; ships are seldom met with in this northern latitude and very few birds; after three or four days one tires of the sea unless used to it; some gentlemen amused themselves by playing at a game like quoits on deck, others walking up and down, sometimes with ladies, and others with reading on deck or in the saloon, which is a very fine one, with four tables which accommodate eighteen persons; there is a merchant on board returning on his seventy-fifth voyage to America; every one who makes fifty voyages by this line is allowed to go free ever afterward; all the officers are Scotch and well conducted; the captain does not keep any one who is not married, or addicted to drinking or swearing; there are chess boards for passengers, in which the captain sometimes joins, but he evidently discourages card playing and drinking; he is a very gentlemanly and Christian minded man, and seemed to take pleasure in having every one comfortable and happy; when not on duty, he often stops and talks to the passengers, entering into all their queries in quite a fatherly manner; Wednesday, the 5th of September, was a most lovely day; in the afternoon the sky was extremely clear and the air light and cheerful; the sun went down in a horizon tinted with such lovely and beautiful colors as are very rarely, if ever, seen in England, but may be seen in the south of Europe; in the evening some of the young men remained on deck for some time to enjoy what they called a Canadian sky and singing:

> " Oh, come to the West,
>   Oh, come there with me,
> 'Tis the land I love best,
>   'Tis the land of the free," etc.

Even when the sun had gone down in this northern latitude at sea,

forty-three degrees north, the cold was quite bearable, though the wind
was against us for days, and the ship's speed was ten knots an hour against
it, steering northwest by north, daily expecting to meet ice floes coming
from the north; some young men posted a notice in the cabin 10:30 o'clock
requiring the gentlemen to muster on deck to form a rifle corps, but it was
the time for morning prayers and singing, which caused it to be a failure;
on Friday, the 6th, I saw five whales to the north blowing and spouting
at about two miles distant; birds begin to be more numerous and varied as
we get near the north of Newfoundland, nearing Belisle Straits; for several
hours we were enveloped in a dense fog, and the steam whistle kept constantly sounding to warn off any ships that might come in our way; hope
to see the first land to-night; saw an enormous iceberg about three miles
off estimated at one-third of a mile long, about one hundred and twenty
feet high and seven times as much under water; the deck was crowded
with spectators, spying through all sorts of instruments, specks, spy
glasses, opera and long short telescopes, at our frosty-faced enemy; it was
quite cheering to see the life and mirth in every one's face at dinner that
day, evidently from the consciousness of having got into smooth water and
the hope of seeing land; as the fog has again returned, we can only go at
half speed, and if a breeze does not arise this evening to clear off the fog,
we will have to keep in the offing till morning, as our cautious captain
will not venture through the strait in a fog by night; he says we have
passed the ocean icebergs from the north, but may meet some small ones
in the lower part of the strait; both water and ship are now so motionless
that one would think we were in a lake or river going at half speed; the
8th of September had a clear calm night, but did not sight Belisle light till
3 a. m.; from 5 a. m. gentlemen were constantly running upon deck to
get a glimpse of land; the Belisle rose high and bold, then, bit by bit, the
Newfoundland coast like little islands, and at times long, low portions of
the island back of the creeks and bays; as we gradually go in, the breeze
freshened very much, and the sailors had to leave off washing the decks to
attend to the sails, while a continued heavy shower of rain finished their
deck work; although we keep near the Newfoundland shore, we can see
bits of Labrador in the far distance; morning prayers over with a better
attendance than usual and a more apparent response to the thanksgiving
for the prosperous voyage; the Labrador coast is now coming in full view
as far as the eye can see, and the Newfoundland, also, but not quite so
high or distant, Labrador coast rising more, some parts bold and rugged,
some hilly and sloping—all wild and uncultivated scrub land as yet; a
brigantine now in sight in full sail going out to sea between us and the
Newfoundland coast; a growing change in the passengers—some waiting,
some looking over the great Canadian chart to find their homes; some
fishing stations and a light house on the Labrador coast are in view, and
the land getting very distant, a long range of vertical cliff-like granite, oc-
casional creeks, in some of which are large masses of ice which look like
large buildings in the distance ; near it and far behind are very high
mountains, whose blue tops look well over the rugged coast line; a Newfoundland fishing lugger (sixty tons) passes close by making for land under
close reefed sails; the sea is very rough and sends nearly all below and
comes over us fore and aft; here can be seen the wonderful power of steam
given to man to overcome the two mighty elements of wind and water.

The sun going down in the beautiful red horizon with clear, etheral blue above. Very strong wind still, the rigging rattling in it and so cold that we have to leave the decks, while in the saloon some of the glassware in the pendant shelves above the tables were thrown out with the force of the pitching and the vibration of the iron ship when the great screw, sixteen feet in diameter, gets out of the water. Sunday awoke in smooth water in the Gulf of St. Lawrence and I felt, when I came on deck for my morning walk and beheld the placid, lake-like sea, the lovely clear sky with the rising sun in all its beauty, that I would willingly travel the same distance over again to behold it. At every service held in the saloon the crew and steerage passengers were brought in; the psalms, hyms and sermon were always appropriate to the occasion, and were evidently felt and responded to by all—indeed, the general harmony that exists between the different clergymen and passengers at morning and evening prayer, as well as on Sundays, might lead one to think that we were all of one denomination, if not of one family, and the great familiarity that exists among the meeting of professions, business men and tradesmen is not less remarkable, but does not lead to that utter republicanism which destroys individual respect for each other. It is an easy familiarity peculiar to the Canadians and superior to what we hear of a large portion of the people of the United States—the latter vulgar and reckless, the former friendly and respectful. While at our lunch news came that a wreck was in sight. Immediately the decks were crowded and glasses pointed toward her. She proved to be a barque on her beam-ends about three miles off on a sand bank opposite the ocean end of Anticosta. They had a flag of distress flying, and our captain sent six men and the chief mate in a boat with a cask of water and a compass, but they did not need them, having only left two days before on her voyage to Liverpool with a cargo of timber. They did not see the bank, so they say, but the case is suspicious, as the ship is eighteen years old and insured, and was in only 13 feet of water, while it draws eighteen. After tea had services again very solemn and impressive and suitable to the occasion. I think we will all long remember our trip with much pleasure. We made many nice acquaintances, the most of them going into the interior. The following is the number of miles made each day: Thursday, two hundred miles; Friday, one hundred and fifty; Saturday, two hundred and thirty-four; Sunday, two hundred and thirty-five; Monday, two hundred and forty; Tuesday, two hundred and thirty-five; Wednesday, two hundred and forty-six; Thursday, two hundred and thirty-two; Friday, two hundred and twenty-three; Saturday, two hundred and ten; total, two thousand one hundred and ninety-five miles in ten days. When nearing land the first novelty that struck us was the neat wooden houses whitewashed, and woodlands with patches of land cleared here and there, the trees of which were remarkably tall, compared to the old country, and not so heavy headed in consequence of growing so close together. On arriving opposite Farther Point in the Gulf St. Lawrence, they stopped to land the mails and telegraph to Montreal the arrival of the steamer. Some of the passengers sent messages to the telegraph office to be sent to their friends. We also sent one to my brother-in-law, Dr. Goldsmith, who afterwards met us at Aston Station. On nearing Quebec, all was bustle and excitement preparing for landing at Point Levi, opposite Quebec. While our baggage was being examined, I noticed one of the passengers take the paper off our boxes and put them on his own to make it appear that his boxes had been passed, (he was a commercial traveler) which aroused my suspicion, but I said nothing for fear of being delayed as witness. In crossing to the train we were surprised to see that priests are allowed here to wear their long black robes the same as on the continent. I was rather disappointed in not being able to see something of Quebec and its celebrated fortress, but had a good view of the citadel in leaving in the train. On our arrival that evening at Aston, we found my brother-in-law waiting for us at the station. We went to Blanchard's hotel, where we stayed till next morning, and left early with a team of horses and wagon with all our trunks and boxes, by a road leading in a southeasterly direction to Richford, six miles from Aston on a fairly passable road, but not to be compared to the roads of England. The appearance of this part of the country was a miserable contrast to the scenery in the old country. The trees were mostly of the fir species and of a very inferior growth, the stumps of the larger ones that had been cut down gave the place an unsightly appearance. Close to Aston the land is flat and sandy, further on rugged and rocky, near Richford more loamy and cleaner. Richford is situated on a small river in a valley at the foot of a steep hill. Went over this hill in a north-easterly direction to East Hastings and crossed a small stream about a mile and a half from Richford. After passing through about a mile of level country, we ascended another hill called McDermot's and at the end of about another mile, turned northwards through a bush road, lined on either side with a dense forest. It was the roughest road I ever traveled, with stones and stumps, roots and mud holes, two of which were very long with water about a foot and a half deep. When about three quarters through this road the wagon broke down. My brother-in-law took the horses and went on to his brother's to get another. After waiting some time we decided to walk on. My wife carried Arthur and I Tom. We had just emerged from the woods when we met a very small woman with a peculiar accent, named Mrs. Cutting. She asked us to come in and rest, as her house was close by the main road. While talking to her my brother-in-law arrived with another wagon and one of his nephews named Richard. They went on for the boxes and we went into the house and waited till they returned and then went on to his brother Herbert's house. He had five sons and one daughter at home, also another son in Montreal, studying medicine with his uncle. After sundry greetings and a dinner we took a walk to see the place. The weather was delightfully fine at that time and we were much impressed with the appearance of the climate, so much dryer and clearer than in the old country. In other respects we were terribly disappointed with the appearance of this part of the country, so rugged and unlike farming land. My brother-in-law's house was what they call here a shanty, made of round logs notched into each other at the four corners. The spaces between the logs were filled with pieces of wood and moss and plastered over with mortar. The roof was of plain rafters with ribs crossways about a foot and a half apart, covered with long, narrow pieces of wood (called long shingles) about three feet long, made of spruce. There are no divisions in his house except one short piece from the front door to the stove. The flooring was composed of loose boards, some of which were broken. There was but one deal table and a

few wooden chairs, and only a loft up stairs reached by a ladder. Next
morning my brother-in-law Richard returned to Montreal. My first experience at farming was cutting wheat with a reaping hook, and before long
I cut one of my fingers. My next was hoeing out potatoes. After that I
began to make preparations for building a house on my lot. I hired four
men living close by, Parker, Cutting, Brodeur and Disselt, at one dollar a
day, and twenty-five cents extra to Cutting and Parker, who could use a
broad axe to square logs, but as the season was far advanced and the snow
began to fall and the logs were unusually large and heavy the men could
not easily lift the upper ones, so I sent to Montreal for a strong rope and in
the meantime made a block and windlass and triangle, which I fixed inside
the house and by that means got up all the logs ready for roofing. The
house was thirty-one by twenty two feet. In the meantime my wife went
to Montreal. The winter coming on, I had to leave the roofing until
spring and my wife returned after seveaal weeks in Montreal. The snow
was remarkably deep that winter, making it a dull life for us, but I had a
little carpentery work in the house and at the stable of my brother-in-law.
In the spring I began roofing my own house. In the month of March,
the weather being rather severe I got an attack of pleurisy; by using proper
remedies I became well in a few days. Next day Herbert and his sons
Joseph and Richard, went to the Sixth range, on the other side of Aston
village, where he ownes another farm which goes by the name of The Lot
on the Track and contains two hundred acres. After breakfast, while Mrs.
G. was milking the cows, the roof of the stable fell down with the weight
of the snow and as the day was warm repaired it, with my nephew Jerrold.
I succeeded in having my house finished by the middle of April, and moved
into it in the beginning of May. I went to Montreal to buy a horse and
was fortunate in getting a good one for forty dollars, with a single set of
harness. When returning in the train I met a Mr. Carmichael with his
wife and family, who were coming out to live on a farm of two hundred
acres, adjoining mine on the west side. When we arrived at Aston they
asked me to wait for them to show them the way through the bush, to
which I consented. They had a horse and cart, a cow and a couple of
calves, fowls, furniture, crockery ware, and five boys and a girl. It
took them considerable time to get ready. When they were, we went to
Richford. It was late in the day when we got there and as they had so
many animals we could not get through the bush before dark. I asked
them to leave the animals at McNeill's till next day, but they did not
like to do so. By the time we got into the woods it was dark and the
eldest boy, who was driving the cart partially upset it, over a stump. It
had hardly been righted when he completely upset it breaking most of the
crockery. After this I drove the cart myself and the boy rode my horse.
While going on in the darkness, an owl began hooting, which so frightened
old Carmichael that he threw himself on the ground, bemoaning the sad
fate of his being brought in the wild wood to be devoured by the savage
beasts that were in it. His wife pacified him and we continued the
journey. We had great difficulty in crossing several pools swollen by the
late rains, some of which were over two feet deep. When we got as far
as Herbert's house old Carmichael would go no further, so I left them
there and went across the fields to my own house, wet and fatigued, it being nearly two o'clock in the morning. Next morning Carmichael came

to me begging to be accomodated till they repaired an old shanty that
had been built on their land by a French squatter. It was seven weeks
before they left my place. While there Mr. C., and his son planted some
potatoes that I lent them, which I got as a bargain from Mr. Cutting,
as he was going to Dudley, to live close to his brother-in-law, Mr. Jim
Dayton, who has a very fine farm in a good state of cultivation. My own
crop consisted of oats, wheat and peas. I sowed a tolerable quantity of
first, but not so much of the others as there was only about three acres
of land on the lot fit for the plough. It was here I handled a plough for
the the first time, with Sim Parker, and I did not find it as difficult, as I
had expected, as the land was free from stones. After
the crop was in, we began to finish clearing the land
that had been partially cleared, but was covered with trees and logs here
and there that had been cut down by a Mr. Brodeur, who had "squatted"
on the lot before my arrival, which means settling on land without pur-
chasing or making any arrangements with the owner.

CHAPTER VIII.

There were very lively times in those days, what with the arrival of
new settlers, "bees" for putting up houses, clearing land, etc., and husk-
ing parties, in which Jim Parker always took the lead. He is a singular
character, resembling Robin Hood on a small scale. He is most of the
time in the woods stealing timber from off the land of absentees, and
sometimes has the audacity to do so from lots that are occupied by their
owners. He is, however, an obliging neighbor and a kind-hearted man,
and gives a great deal of employment to his poorer neighbors, sometimes
employing as much as twenty-five men with their horses in getting out
large pine timber for ships' masts, some of which are as much as eighty
feet long; also crooked tamarac timber for ships' knees, and ash oars. The
tamarac tree is similar to the larch in the old country: these with the making of salts from hard wood ashes, were the chief means the inhabitants
had for making money. They also occasionally peeled some hemlock
bark, for which they received $1.50 a cord delivered at Mr. Sharp's tan-
nery at Richford, where all the settlers on the Third and Fourth range
had to do their trading, as there was only a foot-path through the woods
to Aston village westerly, part of the way through the middle of the lots
on the Fourth range, then in a north-westerly direction for the rest of the
way. It lay across swamps in some places and in the springtime was
almost impassable. Aston was then a stirring place, chiefly caused by
the copper mine discovered some time before our arrival and then in full
work, which employed about 400 men and 200 women. This increase
in population caused great activity in building houses for workmen, stores
and private dwellings. Two private residences were very fine buildings,
built by Messrs. Moffit and Christie, who received many thousands of
dollars for their interests in the mines that were discovered by Mr. Moffit
on Mr. Christie's property. These two gentlemen and a Mr. Lyttleton
acquired a great amount of village property and cut a great dash for several years. One of these was a sort of Beau Brummell and was so fastidious that when his carriage and four were brought out he would pass his

white kid glove over their backs and if it was the least soiled sent them back to the stables to be groomed. About this time I became acquainted with an Irish settler living on the Fifth range of St. Henrie d' Aston. The family consisted of two sons, a nephew and five daughters. They had been working on a railway in upper Canada and had settled on a lot belonging to the British-American Land Company, with only half a dollar in money, after having bought a few weeks' provisions. The lot had no clearance on it when they first arrived. They began by chopping down and burning all the timber on a piece of land and for ready money they made black salts, which they had to carry on their backs to the village of Dudley, six miles off, and sold it to a small storekeeper named Perodeau, which was afterwards bleached in an oven to make white potash. For the first year they lived on potatoes, pork and milk and a little bread, bought occasionally with part of the money made from salts. For several years the work progressed slowly on my place on account of my being utterly unaccustomed to backwoods life and manual labor. At this time there was an application made to the Government to get the concession lines surveyed, in order that a road might be made along it to the road leading from Aston to Richford. At the same time the side lines were altered also. They were moved about one acre eastward and Mr. Carmichael paid for the improvement he got on my side, but Goldsmith was not satisfied with the valuator's decision on his side, which was six dollars. Ultimately I gave them a cooking stove worth ten dollars for it. The first survey of the lines had been incorrect, which was the cause of the delay in making the road; each land proprietor had to make that part of road opposite his lot. The road was made thirty-six feet between the fences, twenty-four feet for the road, three feet for each ditch and three for the bank between the ditch and the fence; each proprietor had to make half the breadth opposite his lot. There were many quarrels between Carmichael, Goldsmith and myself, chiefly caused through want of fences and cattle trespassing on each other's crops. One of the first quarrels was about Carmichael's cattle going into Goldsmith's oats. The G.'s shut up the cattle and demanded compensation. Mrs. C. and her hired man went and demanded her cattle. Mrs. G. put her back to the stable door and refused to give up the cattle till the damages were paid. Mrs. C. objected because the cattle were not shut up in a pound. After considerable altercation Mrs. C. threatened to shoot Mrs. G. with an old horse-pistol she had in her hand. Mrs. G. sent Jonathan, her son, for me. After I arrived I succeeded in pacifying Mrs. C., who was under the influence of stimulants. Her husband afterwards came and paid the damages. Not long after the G.'s had a quarrel with Jim Parker for shooting their horses with salt when they trespassed on his land. I also had several differences with the G.'s and C.'s about our cattle, after which I decided to have the lines run between us. Mr. C., of Montreal, who owns the lot on which he lets his father, step-mother and step-brothers live, was satisfied that I should run the line between. The G.'s, however, would not consent to my running it, so we were obliged to get a surveyor with a license. Mr. C. treats his father and step-brothers in a very liberal manner, having built for them a new house and barn and allows his father an annuity. About this time we expected to have more protestant neighbors, as my brother-in-law in Montreal sold three more lots, No. 25 to Mr. David Wells and the east

half of thirty-three to Mr. Lane, and the west half to Mr. Sherman. The
latter settled on his land. The family consisted of Mrs. Sherman, her
father and mother and one daughter, named Teresa. He paid six hundred dollars for his half of one hundred acres and stayed at my Herbert's
house till he had a house built for himself and a few acres of land cleared.
Shortly after his wife and daughter came from Montreal, much to the
satisfaction of my wife, who would now have society of a more agreeable
character. Having no horse when he first came he sowed his oats in a
very primitive manner, by means of a crooked stick which he dragged
after him forming little furrows into which his wife dropped the oats and
his daughter followed covering them with a hoe; his daughter also helped
him in burning brushwood back of their house, which was exemplifying
with a vengeance the theory of a friend of mine, Mr. Meredith, that of
"from the wash-tub to the piano," as in the evenings, after a hard day's
work, she would play a few tunes on the piano. His house, although
built of logs and of a rude appearance outside, was very tastefully ar-
ranged inside. It had three bed rooms, a dining room and a parlor. The
parlor was nicely furnished, floors carpeted, walls papered, and several
good oil paintings, water colors and pencil drawings, done by himself, on
the walls.

About this time the municipality became divided into three: The
village constituting one, and the rural portion two—St. Henry d' Aston
and St. Marie, the former our parish.

Also, at the same time, Mr. Perodeau, of Dudley, attempted to
divide a portion of our township and join it to Dudley, and succeeded
after great opposition. By this means he strengthened the French Canadian and Catholic votes in Dudley, of which he was a prosperous
inhabitant, and which would aid his prospects and aims. Nine miles of
country in length and seven in width was added to Dudley, which almost
equalized the two hostile parties in that township.

After the subdivision of the municipality Mr. Meredith, superinten-
dent of the Aston copper mines, and a leading person in church and school
affairs, came out to instruct us in the organization of a dissentient school,
and a meeting was called and an election held, at which Mr. Goldsmith,
Mr. Sherman and Mr. Cutting were duly elected as first trustees, with
myself as secretary and treasurer, and the following document was sent
out to the School Comissioners:

"To the Chairman or President of the School Commissioners for the
Municipality of Henri d'Aston in the County of Bradford: Whereas,
the school act at present in force in this province empowers the inhabitants
and landholders of any municipality professing a religious faith different
from that of the majority of the inhabitants of any such municipality to
establish dissentient schools and name trusteee for the management there-
of in case the regulations and arrangements made by said School Com-
sioners for the conduct of any school should not be agreeable to such
inhabitants so dissentient; and, whereas, the regulations and arrangements made by the School Commissioners within the municipality of St.
Henri d' Aston are not agreeable to us, the undersigned inhabitants and
land owners within the above mentioned municipality professing the
Protestant faith, which differs from the faith of the majority of said
municipality who are Catholics, now, therefore, we, the undersigned

inhabitants and landholders of said municipality of Henri d' Aston, so dissentient as aforesaid, hereby collectively signify to you this, our dissent, in writing, from the regulations and arrangements made by the School Commissioners of the said school municipality for the conduct of the schools within the same, and that the same is not agreeable to us, and herewith is given in the names of the three trustees chosen by us in pursuance of the requirements of said act."

Shortly afterward the trustees appointed my wife as school teacher of the new school, which was to be held in my house until a suitable school house was built. She had been teaching a private school, free to all the Canadian children that wished to attend, before this. The French Canadian children now discontinued coming, as a school of their own had been started.

The municipal affairs at this time were in a ruinous condition, and I joined several others in sending the following petition to His Excellency, The Right Honorable Charles Hanly, Viscount Monek, Baron Monek and Governor General of British North America:

"The petition of the undersigned proprietors and inhabitants of the municipality of Henri d' Aston, in the county of Bradford, humbly showeth: That our municipal affairs have been for many years grossly mismanaged, through unqualified and incompetent persons getting into the Councils of said municipality; so much so, that this township is now, and has been for some time, heavily encumbered with debts, notwithstanding that we have been paying for many years a much heavier tax to said Council than any of the adjoining townships, which tax, if it had been properly appropriated, might have considerably reduced our liabilities by this time instead of their having become a most greivious burden to all and almost ruinous to many of our poorer inhabitants.

"That such incumbrances lead, firstly, to lawsuits consequent on the acts of said unqualified and incompetent Councillors; secondly, to loss of public funds in repurchasing lands illegally sold by orders of said Councillors and by the misconduct of their secretary; thirdly, to borrowing money at high rates of interest to meet immediate demands, in consequence of the refusal of many persons to pay taxes, on the ground of the Council being illegally constituted—that some of the first members of this Council and their secretary are particularly reprehensible in these respects, so much so that their transactions were the cause of heavy lawsuits against them and repeated public meetings to investigate their accounts and transactions generally, which ultimately resulted in the compulsory retirement of some of their members, the dismissal of their secretary and the appointment of others more competent.

"That there has been of late years very great difficulty in getting any competent persons elected Councillors of this municipality owing to the intrigues of crafty persons who, not having much real or tangible interest in the township, seek to get in ignorant and incompetent men of no good repute as Councillors, who easily become their dupes and fools, working out their unlawful schemes—such as partiality in the disposal and execution of the public works; and some of the first members of the Council, with the former secretary, are persons of this description, whom it is most desirable for the public good to keep out of the future Council.

"That this Council neglected to have their valuation roll completed within the period, and in the manner, provided within the statute of the municipal act; whereby, no tax could be collected during that year, which made it doubtful to us whether an election of Councillors would be legal or not.

"Under such circumstances some of the former Councillors, together with their former Secretary, seem anxious to get into the new Council the same or nearly the same persons who were in before by means of an application to Your Excellency, through the Mayor of this Council, Mr. J. Daigle, at the instigation of the former dismissed Secretary, E. Fradette, a relative of his, whom we consider the main cause of the mismanagement of our Council affairs by his influence over the majority of the former Council, ——" [Manuscript missing.]

I now have to begin a painful task—that is, to give a truthful picture of my life and those associated with it. I intend to try and have the picture lifelike and keep nothing back from the public except oaths and language that would only fill them with disgust. My earlier days was blessed with the loving instruction of a devoted mother, to whom I owe whatever education I possess. She truly was "a bright and shining light" to the surrounding darkness, and instructed all the English children and many of the French children in all the elementary branches of an English education, besides teaching in a Sunday school regularly every Sunday. It was, however, her beautiful life of gentleness and charity that touched even the hardest hearts and won the admiration and respect of even the most ignorant and worthless of settlers, and truly she was a ministering angel to all that were sick for many miles around our place. Her cheerful words of comfort and the many little delicacies she gave them brought much happiness to many a sick bed. I have often seen rough men instantly stop their coarse, rough jokes and conversation when she entered the room and commence on some other subject, which truly showed the respect they held for her; yet I have seen these men laugh and joke while passing the night in a room with a dead friend. She always exerted a pure and elevating influence wherever she went. I am fully convinced that many times her heart longed for the society of refined and cultivated people, to which she had been accustomed in her younger days: but she piously became resigned to the hardships and privations of backwoods life because she did not have the means to live in the society of her younger days, for her income was only four hundred dollars a year, which she received from her brother in London, for whom she had kept house eleven years before she was married. With this small income she was merely able to live comfortably and keep one servant. Every three months she went to Montreal to receive it, and generally spent a week in visiting her friends there. When there, she attended a meeting of the Plymouth Brethren, to which sect she belonged; but she had broad and liberal views of religion. In her younger days she was a member of the Church of England.

CHAPTER IX.

When fifteen years of age my brother and I rented the farm from my father and had complete management of it. We were very enthusiastic and worked it energetically, making great improvements and finished covering the barn that had remained in an unfinished state nine years, cleared more land, made sugar and sold bark and wood, and often told our dear mother that we would in a few years provide her a home worthy of her, at which she would, with a loving smile, tell us her first wish was that we should become good and Christian men, and that if we became that "all things else would be added unto us." My father, however, did not like our practical farming and took the management from us to resume his theoretical system, which made us greatly indignant; for he often spent as much as fifty dollars in pulling out stumps and stones from an acre of land, which money was advanced by our mother. We thought this was not right; our policy was to make the farm pay for its own improvements, and assured him that land was so cheap in America that it was folly to spend more than a certain amount in reclaiming a piece of land. He, however, would not be convinced, and our opinions greatly clashed together, and we would often have disputes when he would have us work with him for over a day in pulling up a single stump. We told him the right way was to leave time and exposure to such work, and to clear more land would be far more useful and practicable. It, however, only required a sad, reproving look from our mother to bring us into submission. Often in the evening Tom and I would have grave consultations in our own room as regards our future, as to what we were going to do in life, thinking it was high time to begin to think for ourselves, as certainly the home farm did not present very encouraging prospects of our being able to make a comfortable home out of it, and certainly it could never become remunerative under the system our father operated it. My brother Tom finally decided that farming was unsuitable for him, as one of his legs was paralyzed, when three years of age, through his nurse leaving him exposed to a thunder storm in a park in London. He, therefore, with my father's consent, studied telegraphy at Aston with a Miss Frazer, who was operator there, for which he paid the small tuition of fifteen dollars. He learned telegraphy in the early part of the winter of 1876. During this time I wrote to both my uncles and told them I could not possibly waste the best part of my life on the home farm, which, from the way it was managed, was utterly unremunerative. A short time after my Uncle Richard, of Montreal, wrote to me saying he would sell to me and my brother 400 acres of land, known as thirty-four and thirty-five, situated a mile and a half from the homestead. This he thought would be better than for us to leave our mother alone. After due consideration my brother and I decided to buy the two lots from my uncle, paying him the price he asked, $1,200 in four years, at interest. I now give a short scrap of a journal I kept at that time:

April 1st.—Repaired roof of old shanty Uncle Richard built on the lots, when he came from Montreal to live on them for his health. Also cut brush.

May 1st.—Gave F. Buck three acres of land to clear at nine dollars an acre.

May 2d.—Tom and I commence logging.

May 6th.—Herbert Carmichael changed a day with me at logging.

May 7th.—Sunday Jonathan G. and Clifford C. came to see us. It was raining hard. They stayed to dinner.

4

May 8th.—I went to Doherty's and bought ten bushels of oats. Also called in at Meredith's on my way.

May 9th.—Received a letter from Uncle Richard saying that he had sent us a present of a mowing machine and horse-rake.

May 11th.—Went to Aston for the mowing machine, and received an invitation to a party at the Rev. L. C. Willoughby's.

May 12th.—Went to the evening party; had a splendid time; came home at 5 o'clock in the morning and broke the spring of buggy on the bad road.

May 13th.—Went to Aston and had the buggy repaired.

May 14th—Cut brush.

Father became sick. We telegraphed for Uncle Richard. Under his and Dr. Bacon's treatment he became well in a few weeks. Ever after his sickness our dear mother has been ailing, and went to Montreal for treatment, where she stayed somewhat over two months. During this time Tom and I were very busy in working father's farm for him and our own. We cut down all the brush that had grown up in the clearance Cousin Richard made while he was on the lot, also cleared an acre of land ourselves, and then commenced peeling hemlock bark to sell this winter to enable us to pay our installment on the land this winter. The peeling season commenced at the end of May and beginning of June and ends the last of July, or, at fatherest, some times continued to the middle of August. The process of peeling is as follows:

First clear the small brushwood from around the foot of the tree, for men are often cut by their axes striking a small twig and glancing off and striking their feet; then the axeman eyes the tree and calculates in which direction it leans most. His object is to fall the tree on some other logs to keep it from the ground, so that all the bark can be peeled from off it. After the tree is fallen one axeman slits the bark and notches around it every four feet. The peeler peels it from off the trunk and stands it up, which makes the bark of a better quality than if the white surface was left exposed to the wind and weather. Another axeman cuts the branches off and gives a slight cut where every branch was cut off, which enables the bark to come off easier around where the branches were and without breaking. Two to three days of fine weather is sufficient to dry the bark. It is now carried into heaps and piled in cord and half cord piles with the rough side up and stakes on either side of the pile.

While we were thus busily engaged, we received a letter from my uncle, saying our mother was not much better and was going to return shortly. I was much shocked at her pale appearance on her return, but even then we apprehended nothing serious, nor did my Uncle Richard, of Montreal. It was several weeks after this, while she was sitting in an easy chair and I was arranging some flowers on the table, that I fully realized the loss I was about to suffer. I cannot tell you the anguish that filled my heart when she said to me:

"Arthur, my boy, I have not long to live. Promise me now, my dear son, that you will always try to be good and noble and use the Bible as a 'light to your feet and a lamp to your path.'"

I threw myself on my knees beside her and sobbed aloud: "Oh, God! spare the life of my mother. Let me not now lose her to whom I owe such an eternal debt of gratitude. Spare her to me at least for a few years longer, that I may have the pleasure of being her comforter and support."

She consoled me, and said: "My dear Arthur you need never upbraid yourself as being an undutiful son, for you have always been a good and dutiful son to me."

But, at times like this, one's conscience is very tender, and mine recalled many childish acts of disobedience for which my mother tenderly forgave me. I need not tell the reader of the gloom and sorrow that pervaded our home for the week before she died and for a long time afterward. It was on Sunday afternoon at 3 o'clock that she died, on the 20th of August. I lost the best and truest friend I ever had, or expect to have. My Uncle Richard arrived from Montreal, and the crowd of French Canadians that attended her funeral, as well as of most of the settlers for miles around, was a touching tribute of respect they had for her.

I shall now give a few letters that I have collected from my mother's friends, and am sorry that most of them have been lost, or mislaid, and many are illegible, some of which date back as far as 1830.

CHAPTER X.

Fifty-nine Strada, Carlo Alberto Casa Genoa, Italy, 1857.

MY DEAREST SARAH:—I hope you will not think me negligent in not having answered your answer to mine ere this, but I have been so much occupied in and out of the house; however, I am determined not to let another blessed day pass, without wishing you and Jonathan every happiness of the season. May this year be in every way prosperous to you. I often wish myself in your book store, as I always had a penchant for selling. Augustus admires your independent spirit, and begs to be kindly remembered to you. We continue, thank God, to be most comfortable and peacable. Augustus is a kind, good creature, and a highly moral man, and is greatly respected and liked by all here. We have much, my dear Sarah to be thankful for, the Almighty has been very merciful to us, in taking from us one, He has sent us another kind friend, and I trust he may be long spared to us. He was absent, to and fro about a fortnight, forty miles, at a place called Chiavary, where he was sent for to attend the Countess Dunaghmore, an Irish family. She was on her route to Rome, with her three daughters. She unfortunately died, her body was brought here to be buried. It was very distressing to die in a foreign land. Some other families here have been most kind to us, and whenever we go out, we have a carriage to take us to and from any soriee we are invited to, of course free of expense, as you must well know we could not afford it ourselves. We have been at very heavy expense lately with respect to our things, seeing one of the smallest of the cases of poor Jack, fell or rather was thrown into the sea, it slipped as they were hoisting it in the boat. Augustus tells us that the books are soaked, and will of course be marked. A great many of the glass things have been smashed, you may judge of my horror, my poor etagere I fear will look very bare, we are to get them on Monday. Besides all these damages we will have eight pounds duty to pay on all the freight from London, and the total duty on the furniture, books, music and trinkets, will amount to fifteen pounds. So that we must now look to every shilling. We have every comfort, a capital table, beautiful fire, two servants, and nothing earthly to do, not even my hair to dress, as the women do it. We may be as ill as we like, for we have attendance and physic gratis. I do wish, my dear cousin, that I could share my comforts with you. Is there really a prospect of your brother Jerrold entering the blessed state of matrimony? I wish for his soul's sake he would, it would be so much better than flirting with so many fashionable coquettish admirers. I hope Miss Howard is still with you, she seemed just the person calculated for you and Jonathan, quiet and fond of children. I hope this child will be spared to you; I trust all your friends are equally kind to you. How does my aunt look? What a wonderful constitution she has, poor soul. I suppose you all spent your Christmas together. We had two ladies and a gentleman to dinner, after their departure we went to a party to Madame de Knis. I thought of the last party we all spent together, we too had a fine turkey and also a capon for our Christmas dinner. No plum pudding, other sweets instead, we were afraid to attempt one as the foreign cook invariably spoils them in the boiling. The Genoese are as obstinate as their mules. We have got another cook, a Sardinian from the Island of Sardina—she promises fair. I have no news to give you dear Sarah; mamma is, thank God, very very well, with the exception of her constant companion, a cough. I myself was never so well, thank God, though I hardly walk, except to church, as it is not customary here for ladies to walk out alone, so I am a prisoner. Our home is so comfortable, and in such a lively situation, that I do not care if I ever go out. Parties to me are most irksome, I am no longer a *la fleur de l'age* to enjoy them, and am no dancer, so that I enjoy our quiet little tea and fire side more. I long for my piano, which I fear will not be the better for a stormy voyage. There have been an immense number of shipwrecks and the vessel on which our things came had her sails all shattered. Five finger glasses were all in smithers. Mamma was not so successful in superintending the packing this time. Give my love to all our friends and relatives and kindly remember me to Miss Howard and Mr. Frothingham, and believe me to remain, your loving cousin,

L. MODIVILLE.

Montreal, July, '65,

MY DEAR HOWARD:—I have had a sharp note from Mr. Carmichael, also one from Herbert complaining very bitterly of some of your hired men having cut ash timber on their lots. I would respectfully suggest and to stop all further complaints that you ask Herbert and Carmichael to go over their lots, count the number of trees that your men cut, send the amount of their value and I will send you the money by return of mail to pay them. I also think it your duty under the circumstances to write to each a letter of explanation, and I implore you to avoid those disgraceful family broils, which will more than upset any beneficial influence your wife could have with the Canadian people in your locality. With love to Sarah, Tom and Arthur, I remain ever, Howard, yours affectionately,

R. I. GOLDSMITH.

Montreal, 1865.

MY DEAR HOWARD:—I received your letter the day Herbert came

in. I am sorry you did not get my letter in time to come into the exhibition; the show of cattle and vegetable products was very large, but the industrial department was not so good as on former occasions. The horticultural department was also very good. They were shown in three different places, the industrial in the largest place, the cattle on the priest's farm and the horticultural in the skating rink. I intended to send you a paper, but forgot to do so. These houses, financiering, and patients so bewilder me that I do not know what I am doing half the time; the way I contracted for the building of the houses caused me a great deal more trouble than if I had given them all to one contractor. I had a conversation with Herbert about the lines and I regret to say he shows a very antagonistic spirit. He thinks your notice was not according to law. He was anxious that Mr. Barnard's agent would grant a piece of ground to build a school house on. Let me know what Sarah's wish is as regards the matter. Margaret thought it would be a great inconvenience to Sarah, particularly in winter. I enclose you the surveyor's note: ask him whether your note was according to law. In conversation with Herbert he told me about ten dollars per acre was what was generally allowed for cleared land. He seemed to say that he would not give up the land until he was paid. I shall be most happy to advance you the money, it will not inconvenience me to do without it for a few months. His receipt in the presence of the surveyor is sufficient, I do not think you need go to the expense of a notarial agreement, try and throw oil on the troubled waters, with as much discretion as you can. Believe me to remain your affectionate brother   RICHARD.

London, '65.
MY DEAR SARAH AND JONATHAN:—I received your both very welcome letters, I was truly glad to hear that the farm at last is getting on well, but was much surprised at the small quantity of land you have cleared. I also was sorry to hear you say that you did not wish your neighbors to get hold of the breed of your Durham cow. I should rather advise you to encourage and persuade your neighbors to keep good stock as it would make a market about your place and increase the value of your land and have something to leave to your dear children. By the by, you do not mention them lately; I hope they are well. The more your neighbors thrive the better for you. Have you any bees and honey? I suppose not, as the winter is so long. I am glad Richard is building a house near you; it will be great company. What a pity Herbert and family are not more like Christians and live sociably, I cannot possibly realize the idea of people situated as you are keeping up a quarrel. It reminds me of two Irish sailors on the top of a mast wrecked in the ocean fighting about an argument whether Cork or Dublin was the fartherest from them. We have had a miserable winter, sloppy, wet, sleet, wind and cold, so many people ill and dying of bronchitis and lung diseases. The letter closes with news about old friends.

1871.
MY DEAREST SARAH:—Anne Sanford and Mrs. Thornhill and her husband, Colonel Sanford, have just been here to lunch looking in a high state of preservation. I am writing this at dinner, my dear Margaret talking of you to Richard, she sitting at the head of the table Richard at the side with his back to the fire and Rupert opposite him, while I am at the foot

of the table. Richard has just said that Aunt Sarah wears a cap, and it becomes her very much. Margaret wishes me to ask you if you received a letter from her a few weeks ago, which she wrote to you from Leamington. Richard is very methodical and gets up and comes in like clockwork and is getting on famously. Like all Canadians he feels the cold, for Canadians live like Russians, in stoves of a larger size. I hope Jonathan has made your house comfortable, frost and weather tight. A comfortless house is a dreadful misery and generally arises from folly and laziness. Richard, Rupert and I went to spend the day at Lawn House, Lambton, near the Thames, where he met some beautiful and wealthy young ladies but he seems to think nothing of the English compared with the lovely young ladies of Montreal, he is always talking of home and amuses us by his quaint droll stories of Canadian life; he is like our poor good brother Philip. I should dearly like go to Canada in the autumn, in July or August. Thank God my dearest Margaret is better, but she is not well yet. It is a great thing that she is in much less pain than before and I feel that our repeated prayers to our dear Lord have been most mercifully answered and you can hardly picture to yourself the agony I suffered when listening all night to her moans. News of old friends ends the letter.

MY DEAREST SARAH:—Dear Jerrold has kindly left me this small space to fill and I shall do it with pleasure, I wrote to you from Leamington and hope my letter reached you. Richard is expecting to hear from you to-morrow. His account of his life in the woods on lots thirty-four and five has made dear Rupert long to be there. He is most persevering and will I think become a bright star in the medical profession for he allows nothing to interfere with his hours for attending the lectures. You would be pleased dear Sarah, to see how strong and well dear Jerrold is looking, as full of spirits as ever. I am still far from strong but have much to be thankful for to a compassionate and good God. Dear Rupert is pursuing his studies at home with a tutor as the school he went to in the summer is in an opposite situation and it is to cold for him. "News of old friends. He sends his best love to his cousins with mine, with kind regards to Mr. Howard, and fondest love to yourself, ever dearest Sarah your loving sister   MARGARET GOLDSMITH.

MY DEAREST SARAH:—On the other side I send your quarterly allowance. I bless and thank God, that I am enabled to pay it to you punctually. I have also sent to you in his name a present, thankful to our Lord, that so inclined my poor weak heart to feel great joy and comfort in doing so. I sent seventy pounds sterling by a bank letter of credit, but knowing Jonathan's roving habits and his mismanagement, I left it to Richard's discretion as to its use and application, especially as I think it a cruel thing towards the poor dear children to sell the land that will get a safe and profitable home for them to exchange it for a rubbishing cottage or two in a low falling neighborhood. I hope God will act for you in this, and in all things. I trust Herbert is not brutal and tyrannical, he wrote me a ridiculous letter, insinuating that I was guilty of a falsehood, because I said a guinea pig jumped on the table, it did off a mahogny desk, and ate a bit out of his letter; for this he ridiculed my christianity. alas for his poor head, I fear for him. (news about mutual friends.) Love to Jonathan and the boys, good bye, dearest sister, your affectionate brother
                                                   JERROLD.

Letters received from Allen H. F. Robertson, of **New Brunswick.**
My brother Tom made his and his father's acquaintance while going to
Montreal with my mother in the following manner: The Robertson's attention was attracted to a pair of flying squirrels that my brother had in a
cage, a conversation was struck up and my brother gave the squirrels to
them. The eldest Robertson kept up a correspondence with my brother
for eight years and the son for the same period with me, although we
never saw each other.

December, 1870.

MY DEAR ARTHUR:—When I got the nice letter from you and Tom,
I thought I would answer it right away, but I was away from home in my
holidays, and when to school I had no time. I go to the Grammar School
now, and we are going to have our examination to-morrow. I am sorry to
say that one of the squirrels died when I was in St. John's and the other
was so lonely we let it go. Papa saw it afterwards in the garden, but it
never came back; my little brother Robbie is very well and I am very fond
of him. I have got a little sister too, nearly three weeks old. As papa
has written to Tom I thought I would write to you. I send you both a
book as a Christmas present. Give my love to your mother and Tom in
which my mother joins. Your loving friend   ALLEN ROBERTSON.

Fredericton, New Brunswick, 1873.

DEAR ALFRED:—I have been having a very nice time of late, skating
and sliding on the ice, for our field is overflowed and is frozen and makes
nice skating and the river is froze about one foot and a half deep. We are
having a written examination now at our school and are preparing for the
Christmas holidays. I have been keeping rabbits this year, and I have
liked them very much, and am going to fix up a place for them to stay in
in the winter. I am going to send you a paper, called the Youth's Companion as a present this year, thought it would be better to give you that,
because you would think of me every week, I hope you will be very much
pleased with it; is a very nice paper and I and my mother both like it very
much. My little sister Myra is very sweet she can walk quite well and
speak a good many words, Nettie is three years old and her birth was the
second of December. She is very sweet too. What lessons do you learn.
I learn Latin, history, arithmetic, geometry, reading and geography. I
have often wished to see you, and hope I will some day.

Leters from J. Hogarth, a German family sent over from London by
Uncle Jerrold to learn farming on our farm. He was a very energetic and
kind hearted young man, but could not agree with father, and left for the
United States after staying about a year at our place.

MY DEAR FRIENDS:—Your kind letters dated fifth of June, I received
in due time and I really feel ashamed at not having answered them before.
I make common plea of not having had time, believe me, so I will come out
with the truth, and say nothing but laziness, but nevertheless I hope to be
forgiven, and promise better things in future. I was very glad to hear
that you were all well and enjoying yourselves, that everything is progress-
ing except the price of bark, which I am sorry to hear has fallen. If I
was to come back, which I would very much like to do, indeed what I
intend doing in the future, I am still holding the same place and will try
and stay till next spring. The climate here is excellent and agrees with

me very well. I weigh now one hundred and ninety-one pounds, which is considerable more than I ever did before. If ever I should settle down anywhere, I believe it would be in California, and then I would be obliged to have a very nice little wife, who could make home agreeable and comfortable, so that I would never think of roaming around any more. There is nothing like a good home. A young man with nobody in the wide world to give him advice or speak a good word to him, when he is low or discouraged, gets into bad habits very quick and goes to ruin, unless he has character and energy to work through troubles. I say do what's right and you will succeed in the end. I have found that honesty is the best policy. Since I left your place I have seen many hard times, been sick in a strange land without money or friends, traveled through the mountains and prairies half starved and more dead than alive with my feet frozen. And when I got to a town the doctor said he would have to cut them off. I told him I would sooner die first. And now here I am again hearty and well and none the worse off for my hard experiences. Now good bye dear friends, hoping to hear from you soon and with best regards to your dear parents, friends and yourselves. Yours ever sincerely,

FRITZ HOGARTH.

St. Augustin, 1875

DEAR TOM: —I received Mr. Howard's letter with your note enclosed. I am sorry you are having trouble about the school tax, but mistakes will occur. I enclose you last year's receipt which I hope will make things right. Dear Tom I am glad to hear you have left farming, it was such rough work for you. I hope you like telegraphing and that it agrees with you. How Arthur must miss you and your dear mother. I suppose you often drive out to see her, give our kindest love to them all, wishing you all a happy Christmas and that God may bless you and prosper you in all your undertakings. Your sincere friend,   ELIZABETH SHERMAN.

London, 1875.

MY DEAR NEPHEW: —I was much pleased to receive your letter; you can hardly realize the gratification it gives me to find that you are a steady, good and hard working boy. Industry is happiness when united with dependence and faith in God. Even now in my declining years spend comfort as well as profit in early habits of work and zeal. We have two friends that are with us night and day. True friends and constant, ever by our side, than lover more devoted or young bride, yet when one comes the other flies away. For jealous friendship no joint vigils keep. The one true friend is work, the other sleep. I was truly sorry though to hear that you intend to part from your father, for the tie of father and son is strong and holy and you are bound to bear a great deal for your parent's sake, in your efforts for them heaven smiles on you and everything prospers in the end. I myself owe all my success in life to my kindness and care of my mother, God saw my struggles for her so he pitied and helped me. I have already written to Uncle Richard about the land I think it wise to have it. I fear this letter is badly written for I have mislaid my spectacles and can only see dimly, I should think the land a good speculation and with hard work it will be a good thing in the end. One thing I pray and urgently advise that you, your brother and dear and godly mother stick by each other. I hope Tom will be able to earn something at telegraphy altho there is nothing so good or healthy and long living as out door work. My son Rupert is going to the Oxford University; he is going to Oriel college, Oxford, and will be under the care of a good Christian man. He and his mother send their best love to you, Tom, Mamma and your father, and all hope you will be united and be under God, happy and prosperous. I hope to hear from you soon again and see you next May or June. With kindest love to all, your affectionate Uncle, JERROLD GOLDSMITH.

MY DEAREST SARAH:—We received your kind letter, but are truly sorry to hear of poor Jonathan's severe illness and hope it will be of short length, and in the end all for the better, and with God's blessing turn poor Jonathan's thoughts in a better channel, by coming as it were closer to his accounts, may by serious thought and closer and more grave examination of his past errors, and present false doctrine bring him with your prayers and God's merciful help, to a right way of thinking and acting, both as to his own soul and as to his duty to others. The true test of spiritual rest in Christ is our dealings in love with all around us. A tender conscience always at our elbow, is a sure result of God's dealing with his own. I can scarcely imagine a child of our blessed Lord, to be a worry and clog to his neighbors and careless of the feelings and comforts of those near to him. Margaret sends her love to you, so do all your friends. Rupert is on his way home, from Italy, where he has been for his health. Write at once as Margaret and I are uneasy about poor Jonathan. We trust the warm weather will do him good. How fortunate you did the best thing for him, in the very beginning, or he would have died in the first eight or ten days. I hope you will never let the boys sell or change their land, but work steadily at it. I shall be truly delighted by and by, to come and build a house out there and live all together. I have written to the boys, and Richard and his son. With sincere love, your affectionate brother

JERROLD.

MY DEAR TOM AND ARTHUR:—I was so glad to get your last letter, every thing connected with your farm interests me. Write as often as you can. I cannot make out what the machine Uncle Richard gave you is like. Cousin Richard is a steady and clever man; what a pleasure to have him with you. We have just got mother's letter, and are truly grieved to hear of your father's illness. The weather here has turned very hot. Cousin Rupert is on his way home, he was last at Venice, and is now at Milan. Have you corn, oats and root crops enough sown, to feed yourselves and your stock? this should be your first work and then save some of the money which will help you to get all the land you can, by and by, and it will turn into heaps of gold, it will increase so much in value every year. I wish I could send you something useful for the farm, but the freight is so dear, and the trouble and risk so great, besides I suppose duty on everything. Rupert has a bicycle and looks such a height up, he goes along on it for miles at the rate of eleven miles an hour. Rupert is six feet two inches. Your affectionate Uncle JERROLD.

San Francisco, 1875.
MY DEAR FRIENDS:—Your kind letters were received, and thank you for your kindness in remembering me once in a while. Letters from dear friends also cheer me up. I am not quick in making friends here. I have

5

no intimate ones at all. I am very glad to hear that you are getting along
so finely and by the time I come to see you will have your whole lot cleared. According to your letter, grain and vegetables are very high there. I
suppose a man could make considerable money there by raising those kinds
of crops, and especially when that new railroad is built from Sorrel to
Montreal, Aston will be quite a town by that time. I hope dear Tom that
you will succeed with your telegraphing, as I believe it would suit you
better than farming. I suppose you are having it pretty cold already with
lots of snow and frost. Here it is very warm and nice. Next month,
that is November, they say the rainy season commences. I am now nearly a year here, how time flies, I like it here first rate, and am still in the
same place. I will try and be better and steadier now, and quit roaming
around a while, and with God's help get something of my own by and by,
and lay the foundation to a good and permanent home. I suppose you
too, must have grown awfully since I left you. I hope you will send me
your picture in return for mine. With love to you dear friends, and kind
regards to your dear parents and relations, Your sincere friend,

FRITZ HOGARTH.

Montreal, 1876.

MY DEAR SARAH:—I received the post office order for twenty-eight
dollars, also the receipt for the taxes on the lots. As the boys are minors,
it will be necessary to appoint a tutor for them as they cannot accept it in
their own name, while minors. Nor can you as there is no marriage contract. As Jerrold is your guardian and benefactor, and as I have been acting as his attorney here, I must first write to him and submit a copy of the
document for his approval. I do not think he will object when he knows
the transaction will be for their benefit. I have drawn out a copy of the
agreement, which I will submit to a notary and send to Jerrold for his
approval. First the price to be twelve hundred dollars. That I acknowledge having received three hundred and sixty-four; that is twenty-eight
from the boys and three hundred and thirty-six from Jerrold, leaving a
balance of eight hundred and thirty-six, payable in four years at two
hundred and nine a year, bearing interest of five per cent. That I retain
the right of taking twenty acres for my own personal use at the same price
as they pay at any time, that they use the whole till I allot my twenty acres
should I ever see fit to do so. That the property held in trust for them by
Jerrold and myself, be handed over to them when of age, that they have
not the power of selling the property for ten years without the consent of
Jerrold or myself. That they be empowered to take immediate possession
of the lots on getting Jerrold's consent and that no one be empowered to
remove the bark or lumber or use the lots in any way without the boys'
consent, that any money you may advance to them you are to hold a personal mortgage on the property. I remain, with love to all, your affectionate brother. RICHARD.

The only letter I ever received from my dear mother:

MONTREAL, December 4th, 1875.

MY DEAR ARTHUR:—I am so sorry to disappoint you, my dear boy,
but cannot go back until next Wednesday. The dress maker is in the
house, making my dresses, two lovely ones. I have a splendid supply of

things for your father, Tom and yourself, a comfortable supply for the winter. God is good to us my sweet Arthur. I hope you read the word of God, it is the only book that will make you wise and happy. How does the servant boy do his work? Tell him I hope to see the house clean and tidy. Your cousins are coming out on New Years day. Give my love to your father and Tom. I remain your loving mother, S. HOWARD.

MONTREAL, 1876.

MY DEAR ARTHUR:—According to my promise I write to let you know about the lots. Father wrote to Uncle Herbert some time ago informing him of the sale, and it is his intention to write to you, but in the meantime you can work away at them, and I would advise you to go down at once and cut down the brush that has grown up in my old clearance just to make a beginning and I believe the arrangements between Tom and yourself will be satisfactory, you have my best wishes for your success, and I firmly believe that you will eventually succeed by perseverance.

WHAT MY MOTHER WROTE IN THE FRONT LEAVES OF A BIBLE SHE GAVE ME.

"When I can trust my all to God,
In trial's fearful hour,
I can bow resigned beneath the rod
And bless his chastening power,
A light will spring amidst distress,
A fountain in the wilderness,"

BLESSING.

"Blessed is he that readeth."

WARNING.

"Thou shall not add or take from. It is the book in which God speaks."

"No one ever resists the Holy spirit and suppresses the convictions of his own heart without a great increase of sinfulness."

"Form your judgements and conform your actions according to its blessed and holy principles, my sons, and you will be happy in time and safe in eternity."

BRIGHTON, January, 1874.

MY DEAR TOM AND ARTHUR:—I received your letters a few days ago, and write to thank you for them. For the last fortnight, we have been staying here for the benefit of mamma's health. This is a very nice place on the sea coast, sixty miles from London. There are two piers here which extend a long way out into the sea, on the end of which a band plays every day. For the last few days it has been too rough for boats to go out. On the beach are men who hire out all sorts of boats by the hour and also supply bait and lines for fishing. In a short time we caught eighty whiting, you have to row or sail out a mile and then anchor the boats above some rocks, where the fish are in shoals. This is for the line fishing but the nets are used from the decks of small fishing smacks which go much further out to sea, and sometimes sail up to Gravesend, at the mouth of the Thames, and from there forward their cargo by train to London. A fine aquarium has been built here lately, they have two fine specimens of the Octopus, it is a very ugly fish, its eyes are bright, more like a frog's than a fish's, its body is round with eight long feelers with which it swims in a peculiar way shooting itself forward by these feelers, and then allowing them to fall close to the body and trail behind as it goes through the water it has somewhat the appearance of a comet. [Rest lost.] Your affectionate cousin,   RUPERT GOLDSMITH.

MARINA ST. LEONARDS, on Sea, September, 1862.

OH DEAR MRS. HOWARD:—My heart is riven in twain, can you remember anything that my poor, precious Victoria ever said when with you respecting her soul. I am so anxious about the everlasting condition of my beautiful child. If I had been told that Blanche was to go, I should hardly have supposed I could have survived it but now her death seems swallowed up in the more unexpected and extraordinary ones accompanying it. My thoughts are continually and above all three, of course, with my beloved husband. At times I am quite miserable, and quite weak in body. None of the servants can comfort me with the remembrance of any religous observation made by darling Victoria. Poor, dear child, she must have suffered the longest. The children told me they had seen you walking with the Miss Ds., in Hyde Park. I returned to London, but what an altered life. A house in Oxford square has been taken for me. God is very good in the midst of my tributations but he is indeed dealing very mysteriously with me. I want a steady man servant. Trusting you are well, believe me, my dear Mrs. Howard, in deep sorrow, cast down, though not destroyed, your affectionate friend,   JULIA AMELIA BARRETT.

Note. Shortly after the death of her eldest daughter, their house took fire, and her husband heroically lost his life, in trying to save their only child.

LARAMIE CITY, March 11, 1872.

SIR:—I have come to the conclusion to pen you a few words, as I feel interested and anxious to hear from you and family and the rest of my old neighbors. I pray that these words may find you all in as good health as they leave me. I have been blessed with the best of health since I have been in this region, thank providence. I imagine that you are all preparing to make sugar. I wish that I was with you. This region is very severe this winter; more so than it has been known to be for many a year. I think that, according to the snow in the mountains, there will be great destruction along the Mississippi river and its tributaries in the spring. I will tell you what I am doing this winter: I am in the mountains of Colorado making ties, and the prospect is very good as to the business. I have twelve men making ties for me. I had the misfortune to lose one of them the other day. Myself and some of my men had to bury him in this country style—dig a hole in the ground and then wrap him up in his blankets, put him in and cover him up; it don't look human. It is my intention to return to my family in September. I would be very happy if I could hear from Miss Howard and the babes, as I always call them. I pray God to bless you and family. I hope you will have the kindness to write me a few words (I don't think you will disoblige me,) and give me all the news.   Your friend,
JAMES DARKER.

January 1863.

MY BEST BELOVED SARAH:—When I look back on the number of

months that I have allowed to elapse since I have received your very
welcome letter I feel quite grieved with myself, because I have no valid
excuse for so long a silence; not that you are to think for one moment
that I love you the less than when you left us, but partly, perhaps, because
many subjects interesting to you when with us would lose that interest
when you are amongst an entirely different set of persons. When I
received your letter I was nursing my eighth baby with bronchitis. She
had been suffering all the winter from it, and our Heavenly Father took
the little one to His heavenly home. It was a blue eyed baby, gentle
and patient, and her name was Edith Catharine. It was my first trial as
mother in the loss of a little one, but I am thankful I could say from my
heart "Thy will not mine be done." Many thanks, dear Sarah, that we
should be the first to try Mr. Morrison's extract; but you forget that our own
firm only uses oak bark and Mr. Morrison's extract is made from hemlock
bark, so they cannot use it. Mrs. Morrison called and spent this evening
with us. I like Mrs. M. very much, but do not think much of him.
They stop quite close to us, but as they did not know you intimately we
did not keep up the acquaintance, as our circle of friends is as large as we
wish it to be. The extract is selling very well among the tanners. The
most important event since your departure is Tom's marriage. He married Sarah Walker, who for many years admired him. She is a sweet
Christian, unselfish, persevering, loving and firm; plain in face, but a fine
figure and taller than Tom; exceedingly well adapted for him, and at her
father's death will come in for a very handsome fortune. They are living
at Clanmire House, which her beloved mother presented him. She has
been suffering from an attack of rheumatic gout that has gone into her
head. She is anxious about her soul—it hath not pleased God to pour
upon her soul His holy spirit. Oh, what a blessed privilege it is to be
one of the Lord's chosen ones. Mary has tolerable health, but suffers
now and then with her liver. Their little meeting flourished and
increased in number; they have prayer meetings Monday, Wednesday and
Thursday evenings. There are several of the Plymouth Brethren living
about here. There has been a large church built in Sydenham Park,
costing sixteen thousand pounds, and a very good evangelical minister has
been secured for it, which is a great blessing now-a-days when the High
Church party are getting more Roman Catholic in their vagaries than ever.
I do not know whether you see much of the newspapers, but our country
is not as quiet as when you left. The lower masses are ripening for rebellion, and Fenianism is a very unruly power amongst heretics in religion
who stalk abroad and commerce has not been so flourishing since the
American war. You do not say anything in your letter of Jonathan. Is
he still as theoretical as ever. Does he till the ground. Tell us all about
him in your letter. You seem to have very good health, which is a
great blessing. You have your two nice boys. You still have pleasure
in imparting knowledge to others—it is quite your forte. My dear husband has very good health and is still the same dear loving creature to me.
Our children are growing rapidly. Florence is nearly as tall as I am,
very handsome, gentle, patient, loving, domesticated, as you predicted
she would be. (She goes on describing the other eight children, but I
will not tire the reader as a mother's description is always partial.) Do
write soon to us, dear Sarah. We all love you so much. You have not

given us a description of your home. I wonder, dearest, will we ever meet on this earth again. I must now say farewell! with our united, fondest love to you. Kisses for the boys and love to Jonathan.

Believe me to be your ever faithful friend,
ELEANOR A. J. BACON.

Father received a letter from a president af a railway saying he heard from a French judge, a friend of father's, that he was a civil engineer, and offered father the position of superintending the construction of the railway; but father did not accept.

In a letter from Uncle Richard to mother, dated 1870, he says:

"MY DEAREST SARAH:—I send your quarter's money, which is settled on you and your children for life, or such of them as may survive." The letter he had signed by a witness.

MONTREAL, July 1873.

MY DEAR SARAH:— I have just received your letter with a large batch of others from Mabel and Angelica, business letters, one from Aston, Richard, and the last, not least, one from your precious self. I hope you got home safely and found everything all right. Margaret left for Kamouraska, with Flora and Clifford. I shall go down in about a fortnight. Can you manage to go with me. If you can I will pay the piper. If I go it will be in about a week or two —much depending on how I feel. I may take an indescribable longing to see my sweet pet, and, as Jonathan says the Goldsmiths are impulsive, I should go whether or no. As you are aware, Mabel and Angelica are enjoying themselves immensely in England. I fancy they feel a little annoyed with Richard for not looking after them more, but if they only knew what a hard job it was to pass an examination in London, I am sure they would forgive him. Richard is a faithful, hard working fellow. He does not like to get rejected. Tell Mr. Howard I am much obliged for the essay he kindly sent me, and I trust his health is improving. I had a letter from Herbert. The only reply he made to my letter was that it was a sin to be poor, but that it was nor his fault. The fact is I wrote the letter for his wife's benefit, and I hope it will do her good. With much love to Jonathan, yourself and the boys, I remain your affectionate brother, RICHARD.

C. O. Bacon wrote to father, in 1871, applying for the position of school teacher in Aston village. He was hired at three hundred a year. At the present time he is the best medical man in the village. Such are the rewards of perseverance and industry.

MY DEAR SARAH:— I was glad to receive your letter. I have at different times felt surprised that you did not answer mine; so I think it was lost. I am thankful to say my eyes are better; rest from overwork did them most good. What a blessing you are all in good health. I hope your two sons are converted. I thought Tom might have been a minister. I scarcely recollect your son Arthur; I hope he will be a great comfort to you. I think it is very nice to be a farmer. I always admired the country, but of course we like the town also. Last year Sankey and Moody came from America. What an amazing amount of good the Lord made use of them to effect. I was asked to join the house to house visiting, which I did for some months: but, from over work, I broke down and got so ill that I did not know whether I would live or not. The doctor ordered me to take mutton chops, brandy and tonic medicine. When you left England you must have missed your brother terribly. You know, dear Sarah, how sorry we were at your leaving England. My sister said it was like a death, but we have a hope full of immortality that the time is rapidly approaching when death shall be swallowed up in victory. Your nephew, Rupert Goldsmith, is now quite a tall young man, and now I most conclude with tenderest love.

Believe me to be your affectionate friend,

ELLEN BIBBY.

P. S.—When Moody was asked what he was coming to England for he said thirty thousand souls, and here he has had more than double that number. It seems as if God was gathering in his people and that as if Satan was ever busy, knowing that he has but a time to do all the evil he can. Romanism and infidelity are prevalent in London. We have a lady visiting at our house who was a Protestant but has become a Roman Catholic and made her children become the same, but I sometimes have a hope left for the children, one 15 and the other 16 years of age, both Americans. One of them has liked very much to read in the New Testament.

DENVER, COLORADO, 1871.

DEAR MRS. HOWARD:—I wrote you long ago from here, but received no answer. I would like to hear from you and know if you are all well and how you are getting along. I have had very bad luck since I have been out here. I have been very sick since last October, I was in the hospital with typhoid fever. I had also frozen my feet; came very near losing them. The doctor said, when they brought me in, that he did not expect that I would live. Last week I left the hospital, but weak as a cat and awfully lame on account of my feet. You would hardly have known me; I was so poor—nothing but skin and bones. And, then, I had another misfortune: While I was sick somebody broke open my trunk and took $75, and also a ticket to San Francisco worth $85, and a suit of clothes. I informed the police about it, but to no purpose. I will not be able to work before spring. Please write soon and let me know how you are all getting along. Give my kind regard to all friends, and, hoping to hear from you soon, I remain yours truly,

FRITZ HOGARTH.

SALEM, OHIO, 1873.

DEAR TOM AND ARTHUR:—I arrived here three days ago and have been resting myself and writing letters since. It is hotter hereabouts than in Canada, that is to say, the sun shines brightly all the time but the air is not oppressive and it is quite cool in the mornings, besides it is a cool stone house, shaded with trees, in which I am staying. It was very cool and pleasant traveling on Lakes Erie and Ontario. We stopped at Oswego, and in coming through Welland Canal, between the two lakes, while the steamer was coming slowly through the canal, I drove to Niagara Falls. It took an hour and a half driving each way. The falls looked beautiful in the sunshine, and the roadway on the Canadian side

was quite wet and muddy from the spray blowing on to it. In going
up the St. Lawrence I did not see much of the rapids, as the steamer
ascended by the canals. Had a fine view of Bauharnois rapids, with a
steamer descending them. It was a fine sight. There are lots of wooded
Islands on the upper St. Lawrence, and the scenery in many parts is
beautiful; but on the Great Lakes it was like being at sea, except that the
water was almost as smooth as a river. On Lake Erie, at one time, we
appeared to be quite out of sight of land, but it was not so at any time on
Lake Ontario. We landed at Cleveland, where my voyage ended.
Cleveland is a very smoky city not quite so large as Montreal. They
burn soft coal here, which makes the city look black and old. I did not
see anything very interesting. There was a tall brick light house close to
where I was staying. The weather here seems to have been different to
what we had at Aston; there was so much rain that the creeks were
flooded. Hay is not a bad crop here as in Upper Canada. This is a
bad year for apples, but last year was a particularly good one. [Other
personal news and inquiries about acquaintances he made at Aston.]

Very truly your cousin,
E. HOWARD.

SOUTH SEA, PORTSMOUTH, 1869.

MY DEAR RICHARD:—I was dreaming of you all night last night,
and snatch a few moments to write to you before crossing in the ferry
boat to the Isle of Wight, which is opposite our windows. I sent Sarah
her quarterly money. I have settled sixty pounds a year on her, and to
be continued to her children; provided, I do not extinguish the obliga-
tion by paying a lump sum of one thousand pounds at any time I may be
desirous of doing so. I pray God that you and your family are well.
It will be a bright day to me when I can go and see you all. I trust that
poor Herbert will soon be reconciled to Sarah, as those family feuds are
very ugly and unprofitable things and a great and sinful ingratitude to God
for all His mercies, especially so from Herbert, who is so indebted to his
relations for kindness and generosity. I have taken a house next to ours
for my father and mother-in-law at five guineas a week. We expect you
and your family to visit us soon. [Private family news I have omitted.]

Your affectionate brother,
JERROLD GOLDSMITH.

LONDON, 1869.

MY DEAREST SARAH:—Your last welcome letter, received about
three weeks ago, gives us great pleasure, as it told us you were all quite
well—a blessing, which I happy to say, we also have great cause for
happiness. For the last six months dear Jerrold and each one of us
have been in perfect health. Your cousin, George Sanford, has had the
title of C. B. conferred upon him for his attention to the sick and dying
in Japan, and was obliged to appear at one of the levees. I intend
soon to send you Rupert's likeness; he is going to be very tall. I was
sorry to hear of your brother Herbert's opposition to your teaching
school, for I can well imagine how interested you feel in the progress of
your pupils. How kind and good your brother Richard appears to be,
as benevolent and unselfish, I think, as my dear John, who is ever ready

to be generous, kind and good to all his and my relations and friends, and is now acting the part of a true son to my dear parents. God has been very merciful in sparing them to us. My father is over eighty. Rupert sends his best love to his cousins. From dear Arthur's likeness I should say he looks very much like his dear father. With love to you and the boys and kind regards to Mr. Howard, ever, dearest Sarah,

Your affectionate sister,
MARGARET GOLDSMITH.

In another letter to my dear mother, dated London, 1861, she says: "Since you have left Montreal, I fear you will find the cold more trying in the woods than in the city. We have had severer weather here than has been known for many years—the water pipes are of no use, and even the gas pipes are frozen. I dare say you have seen an account in the *Morning Post* of my dear husband's charitable donations to the poor during the time of the severe frost. His kind heart was moved by seeing some of the poor starving creatures attack a baker's shop. When the policemen appeared to be using them roughly, he made the whole crowd come to his house, and he and his two assistants were the whole night employed in giving orders to the baker to give them bread." [Private news that would not interest the public.]

Another friend, in 1861, in alluding to the American war, says: "I hope, dear Mrs. Howard, that the fearful disturbances in America have not affected you. We have often spoken of you in reference to the outbreak, regretting that you were in America during such a scene as doubtless there has been, and which I trust is ended by this time."

ASTON, 1871.

DEAR SIR:—Yours of the 1st of January duly came to hand a few days ago, having gone to New Jersey and back. I am very glad to perceive there is some chance of getting you and Mrs. Howard to come and live in the village, and anything I can do towards forwarding your plans shall be done most willingly. I made an arrangement with I. LaBonte, whereby he transferred to me his house and lot on the Mines road, and I believe it and the land adjoining would suit you, and will let you have it almost on your own terms to have another English family in our circle. Trusting to see you, and with best regards to Mrs. Howard,

I remain yours truly,
TIMOTHY MEREDITH.

In a letter, dated 1870, Uncle Richard says to father: "Your mare I think you have treated judiciously. The only remedy I would suggest is one of rosin, one of black antimony and one of saltpetre rubbed together in a mortar, and give a tablespoonful in a bran mash night and morning. If you had some carrots—they are splendid for horses. I must caution you against glanders, for it is a most deadly and contagious disease, but it is only taken when matter is applied to the mucus membrane, such as inside the lips, nose or eyes: for instance, a horse coughing in your face will give it. I am going out next week. If it would not put you to any inconvenience I would prefer sleeping at your house. I expect to succeed in getting you a servant boy before going out."

Before beginning the period of my life, after my dear mother's death,

6

I shall give a short sketch of the four English families who were our neighbors:

The Goldsmith family consisted of eight boys and three girls. The eldest, Herbert, studied medicine and became a doctor in a town far out West, where he married and made himself a good position in society, and annually sent his father over one hundred dollars. The second son, Richard, fell in love with Teresa Sherman, who accepted him; but, unfortunately, his grasping father had the audacity to ask Mr. Sherman how much he was going to settle on his son-in-law, to which the gentleman replied: "I have only one child and intend to leave her all my property, but I must say I never heard of a father-in-law being obliged to settle a certain sum or amount on his son-in-law;" at which Uncle Herbert became indignant and, with his wife, encouraged his son to break off the match and go to his brother out West. It did not require much persuasion on their part to make him do so, for he was terribly disgusted and ashamed of his parents' meanness. However, if I had been in his place, I would not have allowed their meanness to separate two loving hearts; for, had he acted a noble and true lover's part, Miss Sherman would certainly have married him, for she really loved him. He, however, left her in a cowardly manner, going out West without even seeing her.

The third son, Joseph, fell in love with his brother's sweetheart, but failed to awake any response on her part. He was her devoted lover for several years. I remember one extremely humiliating incident that occurred to him. Miss Sherman called one day on a visit to our house. Joseph was there at the time, and, as well may be imagined, he took the opportunity of basking in the sunshine of her presence; but, before many minutes elapsed, his mother entered with a swoop and grasping him by the coat collar led him out of the house. Miss Sherman smiled with pity and contempt, for she was utterly indifferent to his attentions.

The fourth son was named Jerrold, a very intelligent young man, who became a clerk in a large grocery business at Montreal and had very bright prospects before him, being very much liked by his employer who treated him almost as a child; but, in a moment of folly, he refuseed a request of the proprietor to do some slight menial service while the shop boys were engaged at something else. He of his own accord gave up the place and went West. He became a commercial traveler at St. Louis, but a short time after died of consumption.

Jonathan, Philip and Arthur are to be mentioned in my journal.

Arthur, the youngest, died while an infant.

The eldest daughter died in the old country.

Sarah, the second, a fine looking girl, got married to Timothy Deane, a farmer in comfortable circumstances in Davenport, but, even in her case, her parents foolishly interfered and used their influence in persuading her to accept him. He actually proposed to the father before asking the daughter. She could not bear his rough and coarse manners and left him, coming back back to her parents.

Ethel, the youngest, I describe in my journal later on.

The Carmichael family consisted of four sons and a daughter by the first wife.

The eldest daughter married an Upper Canadian.

The eldest son became one of Montreal's wealthiest manufacturers, His name was Walter Richard.

The second son went through the American war, and then returned, became a married men and worked in his brother's factory.

The third son, Jerrold, also went through the war, and then followed in his second eldest brother's footsteps.

The fourth brother was killed during the Savazzi riots in Montreal.

The family by the second wife consisted of four sons and a girl.

The eldest, Stephen, was a would-be Methodist preacher. I remember one ludicrous incident as regards him. A French Canadian met him one Sunday morning in a lonely part of the road gesticulating wildly, and discovered he was practicing oratory on his way to speak to his rustic audience. He also went to Montreal to work in his brother's factory, and got married there.

Daniel, Herbert and Clifford I shall present to the reader further on.

Angelica, the daughter, was a sentimental little creature who eagerly devoured every novel she could lay her hands on. My dear mother during her lifetime often warned her against it. She, however, would not believe they were pernicious, and she entered into matrimony in a dime novel method—she ran away from her home with a man that had been once a gentleman, named St. George, but now a habitual drunkard. The mother's rage and mortification knew no bounds, for she was under the impression that St. George visited their house to pay his addresses to herself, as she had been now a widow for over two years.

The Cross family moved to Dudley to live there.

Mr. Sherman, who was a skillful mechanic, received employment as engineer and manager of the bark factory belonging to Morrison of the village of Preston, six miles rom Aston. He moved there with his family, and earned several dollars a day. He bought a farm there.

A Mr. Bentley, an Englishman, came to that village looking for employment. He had been an officer in the English army and belonged to a good family, but their entire wealth was lost in the inundation of a mine, and his pride would not allow him to remain in the army when he could not live on equal terms with his brother officers, or live according to their style. When he met the amiable and charming Miss Sherman it was a case of love at first sight, and he at once laid siege to her heart. Her parents took an interest in him, and admired his elegant manners and education, as did also Mr. Morrison, who offered him the employment of working the extract pan, which reduced the liquor to its proper consistency. He had no false pride about him and accepted the position at one dollar and a half per day.

Miss Sherman, who by this time had began to somewhat recover from the base treachery my cousin had shown her, began to admire the manly and intellectual beauty of this perfect gentleman, which deepened into love under his ardent devotion, and ended in marriage.

Morrison's bark factory closed some time after this on account of a lawsuit that firm had with Sharp's tannery at Richford.

Mr. Sherman now received an offer from a Mr. Field, who was agent for a large English company that had two large factories, one at St. Augustine and another at St. Liborie, which he accepted, and went there with his son-in-law.

After a few years Bentley's genius became apparent. He invented a new process for which the company paid him a large sum of money.

Shortly after this the company went into insolvency. Here, again, he showed his business talent. The company offered twenty thousand acres of land, several thousand cords of bark and their factories at half price. He accepted, raised the money and in a few years became a wealthy man.

Journal commenced August 30th, 1876:

August 30th.—Bargained with Lapointe for him to draw fifteen cords of bark to Aston for one dollar a cord; also raked and drew in two loads of oats and cut down oats beside.

August 31st—Cut oats.

September 1st.—Cut oats in the morning, and in the afternoon drew a load of bark to Aston.

September 2d.—Rained hard in the forenoon. I drew stones at the Goldsmiths in the afternoon, while Jonathan and Tom made a track for the sawing machine.

September 3d.—Posted letter to Uncle Richard. Took dinner at S.'s. St. George took a drive with Miss Frazer; it is quite probable that they will get married.

September 4th.—Raining in the morning. Forenoon, underbrushed; afternoon, cut roads to bark.

September 7th.—Rose at 5 o'clock. Uncle Richard came from Montreal; went with him. Uncle Herbert, father and myself explored the stream on lot thirty-five and discovered the rock that obstructed its current.

September 8th.—As it was raining fired at targets most of the day. Received a letter from my cousin Angelica Goldsmith, daughter of Uncle Richard, from Salford, England. She married a large manufacturer of hardware, who lives there. She writes :

MY DEAR TOM AND ARTHUR:—It makes my heart ache to think of you now, without your dear mother. I wish I was nearer to sympathize with you, and I pray God to comfort you both. I got a letter from Mabel yesterday, and she told me how grieved they were at not knowing how seriously ill our dear aunt was, or they would have gone out. Poor papa feels it very much. We know that dear in the sight of the Lord is the death of his saints, and what a world of care your dear mother has passed from. Still, for ourselves, our loss is very great. I shall always feel a deep interest in you and would be so glad if you felt inclined to write to me at any time. I think you know my address Oxford House, Salford, England. How is your papa now? I heard that he had just recovered from a dangerous attack of congestion of the lungs. Good bye, my dear cousins, with much love your affectionate cousin,

ANGELICA E. FOTHERGILL.

September 13.—Uncle Jerrold, who had just arrived from London, came out from Montreal with Uncle Richard. Next day we went over Uncle Herbert's, father's farm and our own, and in the evening Uncles Jerrold and Richard went to McNeill's and made a handsome present to Mrs. McNeill, who attended on my dear mother during her illness. Uncle Jerrold generously tries to hide his great grief and sorrow. He only heard of her death when he landed. I can imagine the shock it must have been to him, full as he was of joyful anticipations of meeting a sister he almost adored. In the evening he related to us some of his adventures while serving in the English Legion that fought for Queen Isabella of Spain.

September 16th.—Visited most of our friends in Aston.

September 18th.—Had a dispute—father acting a very mean part to the man who had been a great benefactor to our family since it has been in America. Uncle left in a Pullman car the same morning for Montreal.

Setpember 19th.—Carmichaels came from Montreal and went out shooting partridges. The season commenced on September 1st. During this time we were very busy cutting and cording bark and cutting buckwheat. One evening a meteor fell close to the house. A Frenchman said some one would die in the house before the year was out. Gave out a few small jobs to Canadians to clear land our lots.

One morning Tom and I awoke and found in our room the following that had been written by father for us.

REFLECTIONS.

"Let not soft slumbers close your eyes, until you have recollected thrice,
The train of actions through the day, where have my feet chose out their way;
What have I learned where e'er I have been, from all I have and from all I have seen
What know I more that's worth the knowing, what have I done that's worth the doing,'
What have I sought, that I should shun, what duty have I left undone,
Or unto what new follies run.
These self inquiries are the road that lead to virtue and to God."

This without doubt is excellent advice, but I must say that a single word from my dear mother had more effect on Tom and myself than all my father's theoretical advice put together. The first of October I went to church and took dinner at Guernsey's. It is a Norwegian family, the father was killed in the American war, the wife receives a pension and the three children till they were of age. Tom and I had a dispute. He was trying to get the fall ploughing done before the frosts set in; he wanted to saw wood for the Carmichaels, he threatened to return to telegraphy; measured and inspected the two acres of land, that Ietreault and Lapointe had chopped, also the acre Napoleon had chopped. In inspecting land that has been chopped ready for logging, one has to very carefully examine it to see that the brush piles are well piled and compact or otherwise they would not burn, also that all the timber is cut twelve foot long, if cut longer than that it is too heavy for a team to draw it; also to see that all the logs are cut completely through and that the brush is cut close to the surface of the ground.

In the evening I wrote to Uncle Jerrold, Tom to Mr. Robertson, of N. B. Paid the men for their work, had a dispute with Ietreault because he would not take some sheep that he promised to in part payment for the work. Will not give him any more work. Received a letter from Uncle Richard.

My Dear Boys:—Your Uncle Jerrold left on Wednesday, the second of the month for England, by way of New York. From what he said while he was here, I thought he expected to hear from you. I would advise you each to write a letter to him, enclosed in the same envelope, thanking him for his great kindness to you. I was sorry to hear that your father quarreled with him; even if your uncle was at fault, I think from his former acts of generosity to your dear mother, he ought to have been more careful. Your uncle went to several marble yards, but did not find one to suit. He ordered me to get one. Before sending it out, I will write to you, I think it will be necessary to build a basement for it. Your uncle told me to tell your cousin Richard, to build a fence around the lot and send me the account; should you see him, tell him not to put up the fence

till the headstone is first put up. I do not know what rule there is in
Aston as regards lots in the cemetery, in Montreal they are very expensive.
I think you had better find out from Mr. Willoughby or some of the
church wardens. You might also ask what kind of a foundation
of cedar, or stone. I should like you both to come to town and spend a
few days with us, when you have time. Your aunt is anxious to see you
both. I do not think a few days holidays will do you any harm. Have
you all your crops in yet? Are you going to build a barn on the
lots this year? Have you decided on the place to build the house and
barn? I hardly think it would be wise to have a barn without a house, as
the people would be likely to help themselves to its contents. With love
to your father, believe me to remain, dear boys, your affectionate uncle
RICHARD J. GOLDSMITH.

Went to Mr. Meredith's; paid him a dollar and fifty cents for quarter
of a year for our pew in Aston church, played cards with Florence, Margaret
and Tommy Meredith, came home late, went to church next day on horse
back, passed aunt Margaret and Jonothan at Lefevre's, put my horse in
Mousseme's stables, had a very long sermon, met Nicholas Meredith at
church, on returning home had for dinner, apple pie, potatoes, butter, bread
and milk. On Monday sold Francis Burke a sheep for three dollars and
seventy five cents, also gave him an acre of land to chop for five dollars.
Tom set the sawing machine at C's. The ground is first leveled and large
wooden stakes driven into the ground to which the machine is fastened by
chains. Gave Louis Brodeur four acres of land to partially clear on the
south east corner of our land. He was to underbrush it and chop in
lengths and put in piles all the soft wood timber on it, the hard wood to be
left standing, to be chopped up for cord wood in the winter.

October 10th.—Rose at half past five, milked the cow, during the
day Tom and I dug twenty three bushels of potatoes. Received a letter
from Uncle Jerrold.

MY DEAR TOM AND ARTHUR:—I leave Montreal to-morrow by
steamboat for Toronto to the Falls of Niagara and then home by New
York. It would have given me great pleasure to have seen you, my dear
good boys once more before I slept, but I thought it better not to waste
your money, and still more precious time by traveling, every hour is now
valuable, and gentle, but constant work and employment, is the great secret
of wealth, health and happiness. I shall be glad when you have cleared
and drained some land on your own lots; and then get up at first a small
barn, but one to which you can add as occasion requires. What a blessing that you have a large quantity of land, and that every improvement
lasts forever and adds to your wealth and independence. Every foot of
your land will be more than gold and it is employment which improves
your health and strength. The year your cousin Richard Goldsmith
spent on those lots, saved his life, and I feel assured that if either of you
were confined to any sedentary employment you would lose your health.
May the Almighty God grant that I may be long spared to look after you
and help you on my dear children, and may the good and merciful God
keep you straight in the paths of rectitude and holiness through the blessed
propitiation our Redeemer and loving Saviour Jesus Christ. I should like
some way of writing to you in the future so that your letters may not fall
into your father's hands and although I always wish you to be kind to him
I think it will be best for him and you, that you should act and manage

for yourselves, otherwise if he goes on as he has done for the last fourteen years you will be in want of the common necessaries of life, if anything should happen to me. I feel certain that you will make that a valuable farm, but mind do not strain or over work yourselves, only go on steadily, surely, but diligently and always rely on the unutterable love of your true friend   JERROLD.

October 11th.— Rose at half past five, milked the cow and swept and dusted our room. Finished hoeing out the potatoes, have about seventy-five bushels in all. Ethel came and borrowed some tea. Sarah took tea with us. Jerrold Burke has been sentenced to four years imprisonment for beating an old peddler with a club in a lonely road. Frank Dodsley, Tom and myself swamped eight cords in one day, and made the roads. Father had the cow milked and tea ready on our return. Bark cannot be swamped in wet weather, as it spoils the bright yellow color of it and covers it with spots of mildew.

Sunday 15th.—Posted a letter to Uncle Richard and his daughter Augelica, in England. Went to church on horseback, when I came back, Ethel and Sarah were practising riding. Philip enlivened the evening by playing sacred music on his violin. I read Rifle Rangers, by Magratt.

17th.—Went to a bee to raise Louis Brodeur's house, and make it higher. Used long poles as levers to raise it. Went to school in the evening, Jonothan J. is teaching it. For several days after this chopped cordwood on our lots.

20th.— We hewed pieces of cedar to put under the tombstone that has arrived. Asked father to lend us fifty cents to hire a man to help us to put up the tombstone, but he refused. Uncle Herbert, Tom, Jonathan and myself went to Aston, found that the other headstones were placed on a stone foundation. I went to the mines and got permission from the manager to get a load of stone. We got a stone mason and four men to help us to put it up. Borrowed an old pot at Willoughby's, to melt the cement with which to cement the headstone into the block of granite. Received a letter from Uncle Richard.

MY DEAR BOYS:—We received your welcome letters. I think you are right in not coming in till the fall ploughing is done. As soon as that is over we expect you both in town, as we think a little change will do you good. When you decide to come in, drop me a line. We were glad to hear that Uncle Jerrold's steamer arrived safely. I suppose in about a fortnight we will get a letter from him. I have drawn out a plan of a barn but will show it to you when you come in. I do not think it would be wise to build it until you are living on the lot, as during your absence it might be liable to a number of accidents. Your Uncle Herbert left on Wednesday, we all thought him very much altered, he looked very much older when here. He scarcely ever spoke. I fear he is greatly troubled about his daughter. It is a sad thing and I think more seriously of it than they are disposed to do. I hope with God's blessing, she will see the necessity of going back to her husband again. I explained to Uncle Herbert how the headstone should be put down, I think it will be better not to have the fence too high, and if cedars will grow there, a nice cedar hedge would look better than a rail fence. If it is fine I shall expect you in on the thirty-first, but as much sooner as you like. I would advise you to keep a book of wants and get a three months' supply when you come to

town, bring in a list of your debts, also bring in any clothes that you may
want mending and I will get them done for you. Bring in the zinc trunk
with you for your clothes, and a box for groceries, that is if you decide on
getting them here. Have you got the size of the lot from the church
wardens, if not sixty by twelve would do. Good night, with love to your
father in which we all unite. Your affectionate uncle,

R. J. GOLDSMITH.

While passing the station saw a notice asking tenders for a contract
to supply the copper mines with two thousand cords of wood. Wrote to
Mr. Hogarth and uncle Richard.

25th.—Ploughed at G's., all day. We are changing time with them
which they are to pay back in the winter by helping us to draw bark. Sold
a sheep to Vincent's. The Goldsmiths have taken the contract to furnish
the copper mines, with second growth, ash timber to make pick handles.
Tom had a dispute with father. The G's., have hired Mr. Grant's threshing machine. Tom and I went to Aston next day. Received a letters from
uncle Richard saying if we wanted any money, to let him know, also that
they were expecting us in every day. Started for Montreal at half past one
on a mixed train, reached Montreal at seven. Arrived at uncle's just in
time for tea. Received a warm welcome from Mabel, Richard, my uncle
and aunt; cousin Clifford was not in at the time, had gone to see his cousin
Algeron Hayston start for Hamilton, where he had received an appointment in a bank. Had a long talk about our future prospects and retired
late. Next day Tom Clifford and myself went up McGill College avenue,
saw the new reservoir and ascended to the top of the mountain. We went
to Fletcher's field to see a volunter review. Next day Clifford went to
school. Uncle Richard, Tom and myself had a talk on business and settled
our accounts. In the afternoon I played La Crosse with Richard and
Clifford; also went to the museum, where there is a fine collection of stuffed
birds, fishes, and animals, also warlike weapons, minerals and other interesting specimens, among which was an Egyptian mummy. In the evening
played Chess and Draughts.

November 3rd.—Richard vaccinated Tom and myself. After dinner
went for a drive with uncle Richard; saw the Court house, Nelson's
monument, the Drill shed, the wharf, and all the ships. Drove up Beaver
hall hill and saw Hotel de Dieu, a Catholic hospital of immense size, but
little architectural beauty; drove to Mount Royal cemetery, its numberless
stately avenues, its great extent, densely covered with fine monuments,
cedar hedges and ornamental fences, the bright green closely clipped
grass, with gravel walks winding in all directions, justly entitled it to be
called a beautiful city of the dead. I was thoroughly disgusted with the
Catholic cemetery, its monotonous rows of crosses, and the shabby appearance of it in general. Next day Tom and myself went for a walk; saw
the Windsor hotel, also St. Peter's, which is in the course of erection, said to
be exactly one quarter the size of St. Peter's at Rome and on the same plan.
On the fourth we returned, father met us at the station. On Sunday went
to church spoke to Mr. Meredith about the size of the lot in the cemetery,
took dinner at Wheeler's.

On Monday planted a cedar hedge around my dear mother's grave, also
some fine trees at the corners of the lot. Tom, Frank Dodsley and myself,
with our horses, changed time with Gs., at threshing with the new

threshing machine Grant has invented, which, however, is not a success, as it takes too much power to work as much as eight horses, and is always breaking. Some days only threshed enough to feed the horses. Napoleon wanted to get work from us, but would not work for orders on stores.

13th.—Went to Aston, posted letters to uncle Richard, Jerrold and Mrs. Sherman. Beceived a letter from Mr. Sherman.

My Dear Tom:—I received your letter yesterday. Mr. Sherman cannot come to help to divide his half of the hay on our lot, but says you can give him what you think the hay is worth. The taxes are out; would greatly oblige us if you would pay them out of the money you have to give us for the hay, the rest of the money can stay with you till the lines are drawn in the spring. Dear Tom, we are all very sorry for your loss, in losing your dear mother. You lost at once mother, companion and friend. I can imagine how lonesome and lost your home looks, without her. Arthur and you must try and follow her teachings to be to each other what your dear mother would have liked you to be, had she stayed with you. Tell Mr. Howard we were all very sorry and sympathize with him. I tried to write to him, when I heard of your dear mother's death, but felt so bad that I could not find the right words to say; everything I wrote seemed so cold and unmeaning, to the great grief I knew you must be suffering, that I could not send the letter, but I assure you I thought and prayed for you all. As soon as I heard of your dear mother's death, I wrote to Sarah. She felt very bad about it, and was so sorry that she had not been able to see her when she was at your place last spring. When she was in Montreal she called at Dr. Goldsmith's, hoping to see your dear mother there, but she had left for the station a few minutes before. I thought to write you a longer letter, but the man is waiting to take it to the station. Some of us expect to be in Preston sometime after New Years, and will try and go to Aston to see you. The factory here has not been working since last May. With love to your father, Arthur and yourself, I am, dear Tom, your affectionate friend,   Elizabeth Sherman.

St. Augustin, November, 1876.

FREDICTON, NEW BRUNSWICK.

My Dear Tom:—I was much surprised and grieved to receive your letter informing me of the death of your dear mother. Her death must have been a great loss to you, and I feel sure she was one of the best of mothers. I remember very distinctly our meeting in the cars and how much I was impressed by her conversation, I always hoped to meet her again and become better acquainted, but that can never be in this world; she is now where all is blessedress and light; I feel that she was a sincere Christian, and that her influence on all who came within her reach, must have been good. I would like to hear from you whether you are still in the telegraph office and what your intentions are in future. With the sincerest of sympathy, believe me, your friend truly   A. J. Robertson.

Many of my evenings at this time I foolishly spent in playing drafts with Louis Brodeur. Frank Dodsley since my dear mother's death is learning fast to swear from the boys in the neighborhood and often tells objects and beings, when they displease him to go to a region where the temperature is said to be hotter than that of the hottest tropical country.

16th.—Threshed all day at G's. Threshed twelve bushels in the forenoon

7

and forty in the afternoon, Measured half an acre that Magloire Vincent chopped, there not being quite half an acre, gave him an order on Monsson's store for two dollars and thirty cents. On the afternoon of the eighteenth went to Aston, saw the bishop of St. Jean and Charlesbourg: on arriving they were met by the mayor and a large crowd of people who conducted them to a covered carriage. All the windows along Main Street were liluminated with candles. Delage had a large bonfire made by burning tar in a barrel. On passing Roussin's store a salute was fired; on reaching Moussear's store the band began to play. Went to Richford, paid our bill at McNeill's store, slept at McNeil's. Went to hear mass, next morning at Mrs. McN's. request, heard a combination of French and Latin, also the auctioneering of hens and geese at the church, besides the sale of other articles, also heard miserable music. One day while walking past Sherman's house met Edmond Racine with a rope on his arm; suspected that he was going to steal hay, as we had missed a great deal already, continued walking on as if going home and then returned and watched him. Saw him wrench a board off the window and go in, I followed and jumped in brandishing my axe; he yelled "Mon Dieu" and rushed past me and escaped. The same night I slept in the house on the hay with Carlo, our dog. Next morning I found Racine's cow and horse grazing on the after grass. Brought them up to their house and told them to keep them at home or they would have to pay trespass. It injures a meadow to allow animals to graze upon it, for the "after grass" protects the roots from the frost. On the twenty-fifth decided to have Gs., thrash our grain with Grant's mill, also bargained with Vincents to cut and skin one hundred saw logs. Also received privilege from Vincent, to cut all the hemlock logs we wished on his lot in the third range close to the county of Sussex, Commenced playing drafts French way, with Louis Brodeur; there are sixty men instead of twenty-four. The men take backwards and the king has exactly the bishop's move in Chess, excepting that it jumps over a man when it takes it into an empty square on the other side.

26th.—Went to church, Rev. L. C. Willoughby sick, Mr. Meredith read a sermon. Dined at Wheeler's. Read the Vicar of Wakefield. The roads are rough, the ruts made in wet weather are frozen. Had a dispute with father, he wanted to charge us for Frank's time, who is a mere boy, which we thought ridiculous, as we were providing the house with all the necessities it required. Father said he would write to both our uncles and stop our working on our lots. During these days we cut saw logs. One has to be careful and choose sound timber without too many knots in it. We sawed on an average, forty-one logs a day, but there was much waste in timber. Under favorable circumstances, somewhat more than this can be cut.

December 4th. --Tom and I cut one and three quarters cords of wood which is fair work for us under the circumstances.

7th.—Gave Joe Vincent the job of cutting twenty cords of cord wood at fifty cents a cord, also to pile all the brush and cut any timber that would not split into twelve feet lengths. Nalopeon wanted to sell us his piece of land thirty acres, eight cleared, a log house on it for one hundred and thirty dollars. Father proposed to sell his place for seven hundred dollars, and buy Napoleon's; I however, thought we had enough on our hands for the present. Tom brought the news that Moussean had failed. Our usual diet these times was bread and milk, with sometimes potatoes, herring and occasionally a little meat. One evening I called at Carmichael's, the old woman was setting the table, when I entered, but stopped immediately. I thought it very mean, and determined to tire them out, read novels till eleven o'clock. At a quarter to twelve Mrs. C. finished the operation and asked me to supper; I refused and went home, decided that I had over-taxed a neighbor's hospitality which to say the least is not unbounded. Grant's mill was a failure, the belting was always breaking. When we decided not to have our grain finished by it, as we could have it thrashed cheaper by flail, Philip and Walter were very angry, and challenged me out to fight, which I refused to do. George Barclay came to see us from East Hastings. Herbert C., called at the post for us, received a letter from Mr. Hogarth.

My Dear Friends:—I duly received your kind letters announcing your dear mother's death; it was sad news indeed, and grieved my heart to read it. Believe me my dear friends, I sympathize with you for the loss you have sustained, you have lost the best of friends, a good kind loving mother and no friend however dear, can ever take her place; but kind words expressed by sympathizing hearts will help you to bear up under the affliction. Your kind relations are with you, and will help you through. I can imagine how lonely you feel in the back woods; I should think you would prefer town now. I would like to come and see you and cheer you up as little, but that cannot be, so I hope these few lines will convince you of the sincerity of my feelings. I would have written sooner, but was prevented by an accident that happened to me three weeks ago, from the effect of which, I am still laid up in bed. A team ran away with me, I had two ladies in the carriage with me, we were all three thrown out, I got my leg under the wheel and got it badly mashed. One of the ladies fell on to my back, and tried the strength of my back bone, which stove it in wonderfully well, which kind of makes me think that whale bone composes part of my frame. This lady did not get hurt which is no wonder, considering where she lit. The other was more unfortunate, she struck her shoulder on the ground and dislocated it, for which I was very sorry. The whole cause of the accident was a rotten pole strap, which broke, going down a hill and let the carriage on to the horse &c. The boss thought they were good enough for a while, yet begrudged five dollars for new ones. Now the affair may cost him a thousand dollars. He is honorable enough anyway to take the blame on himself, and treats me very well. Likely by next spring I may make a change again. With love to all, and wishing you all a merry Christmas, your sincere friend, FRITZ HOGARTH.

13th.—Rose at five, breakfasted at six. Andre Larivere came to get us to cut shingle wood into blocks ready for splitting. We give him one dollar for cutting the shingle wood with us, after which he is to make twenty-four cases of shingles at eighty cents per case. A case contains one thousand shingles, averaging four inches in width, and fifteen inches long, which will cover ten feet square. We tried to get pine timber but could not get any that would split well enough for most of the best pine timber has been taken from these parts. Andre can tell to a nicety, whether a tree will split well or not, by looking at its bark. The roads are very bad, several habitants who attempted to draw wood to Aston, had to unload part

of their roads at bare places in the road. Next day, drew four loads of hay
from Mr. Sherman's house to father's barn. Sold twenty cords of tamarac
to Cicero Vincent, at ten cents a cord, that is the cut of it; he wanted us to
trade a mare we had for one of his, if we would give him twenty dollars'
boot. In the evening I wrote a letter to uncle Richard, Tom wrote to
aunt Maria, fourth eldest sister of my father, an old maid, who lives with
uncle Timothy at Waterford: we also wrote to uncle Jerrold, also to Mr.
Hogarth.

MY DEAR MR. HOGARTH:—I received your welcome letter, and was
sorry to hear of the accident that happened to you, but hope that you will
be well again in a few weeks. Forget whether I told you in a previous
letter, that we bought thirty-four and thirty-five from our uncle Richard,
for twelve hundred dollars, that is three dollars an acre. Now
that our dear mother is gone, we will, of course go and live on the
lots. Firstly on account of the distance, a mile and a half to go to and
from work, and other reasons of which you well know. We have prepared
for building and have one hundred saw logs ready for the saw mill, which
will give us about twenty thousand feet of lumber, which will be sufficient
for the house and barn. We are also having twenty-four cases of shingles
made to roof them. We have about ten acres cleared already, and sown
with hay, and about twelve more chopped ready to log. We fortunately
have a double sleigh, wagon, double harness and one horse to start with,
and two good uncles to back us in the bargain. We will try our luck at
farming for a few years anyhow, and I am pretty certain it will be a success
as thirty-four and thirty-five have very few stones on them. At present we
are chopping cord wood on the land we have cleared. Cord wood is very
cheap here, at present only one seventy five a cord, but still it pays better
than to burn it on the land. Although it is the sixteenth of December we
have not had any snow of consequence as yet. I hope if you leave your
place you will get another good one, or that if you start in business you
will succeed. I suppose California is a grand country and has a splendid
climate. I wish I owned a few hundred acres there. Father is a little
more industrious of late as he sees that he will have to trust to his own
efforts to develop the resources of his farm. I regret to say that duty alone
is the only incentive that governs all our actions towards him, and makes us
avoid as much as we can having disputes with him. I hope when you come
and see us you will find our farm and buildings in a better condition than you
found the home farm in the spring of eighteen seventy. Mind before you
leave your place, that you write to us and send us your new address.
I ping you will spend a very happy Christmas, I remain, with much love
your affectionate friend.   ARTHUR N. HOWARD.

Received a letter from uncle Jerrold.

LONDON, December 2nd.
MY DEAR TOM AND ARTHUR:—I have read with much pleasure,
your kind and nice letters, and while I receive with great satisfaction anything connected with your interests, which are very dear to me, I am sorry
that my advice to you from want of knowledge and experience cannot be
of so much use as your uncle Richard's, to him I have for a time given over
all the authority of my tutorship, for three good reasons. First because he

has more sense than I have, secondly he has had more experience in the line of life in which you are placed and thirdly because he is on the spot and can act quickly. As far as I can judge it will be well if possible to keep on with your father and assist him in every rational and useful work. At the same time both for his sake, and your own, you must not be diverted or turned aside by any mortal from making your four hundred acres fit and able to keep you both; in this above all things be united and firm, and under God's blessed help I shall be enabled to see you with my assistance become independent. How glad I shall be to come and see you, on your own cleared farm, and bring your aunt and your cousin Rupert with me, and spend a happy time together; please God it will come yet, but now speaking as a business man I cannot help saying that as yet up to eighteen seventy-five I am disappointed in seeing such a ragged and ill conditioned farm as your father's after so much time and money being spent on it. I hope that I am not unjust in giving this opinion and that I do it in error, in ignorance of what I am talking about; but still so it seems to me. At all events my dear good boys I am sure you will do all you can and never mind the rest. Leave all to a merciful God who will take care of you and enable me to help you and be your friend and uncle in the place of your dear good mother, whose earnest prayers to heaven for you, all her whole life, her loving and devoted life to her dear children, will be heard. Mind you keep yourselves warm, and get plenty of blankets out from Montreal. Do not remain in your wet clothes after work, if ever so tired change them. If you want any thing, do not be mealy mouthed or doubtful, but ask uncle Richard for it like men, and he will do it. God bless you, and make you good, united and happy, my dear nephews, is the wish of your loving uncle Jerrold. I am glad to find uncle Richard has invited you to his house, of course one of you will have to go to Montreal every three months, to receive your quarterly allowance. Go and see my brother Herbert and my neice Sarah, and give them and Mrs. G., my love. I will write to them soon. I need not, I hope, warn you against all quarreling, ill will or neglect of duty towards your neighbors. Remember that one evening can often ruin a man, where one hundred friends cannot save him; and also remember that the greatest cowards, and the worst and vilest men, are the most quarrelsome, and the most ready to take offense; to be angry and revengeful is devilish, to be kind, patient, slow to anger and good to those that hate you, is Godlike.

Went to Mr. Willoughby's, had quite a confab with Mrs. W., about my cousin Sarah leaving her husband, Timothy Dean, for such a trifling cause, that of being over worked which is often the unfortunate female's lot on large farms. In my opinion, she acted in a spirited manner, in not becoming a slave, when her husband had ample means to hire a servant. To be industrious and economical is all very well, but to save a hundred dollars a year through over taxed energies and a ruined constitution is to say the least a most false economy, as no doubt many farmers wives throughout the country find to their cost, when it is too late. As I was passing Mrs. Wheeler's I noticed their chimney on fire, told her of it, she very composedly sent her son Justin for a pail of water, and put out the fire. This woman is a model wife and house keeper, although her husband receives but small wages; they live in a cosy little villa, which is beautifully furnished, inside every nook and corner of it showing the artistic and refined taste of his wife, who is cook, housekeeper, housemaid and dress maker all combined, yet although she does all this work, and is rearing a large family of six children, she is always neat and well dressed and ready to receive guests. Truly happy are the men who are blessed with such wives as these. Came home like the wind, and was nearly frozen, it was so cold. Happened to see a letter from Aunt Maria to father, amongst waste paper and was mean enough to read it. He has been writing to her, saying how mean it was of us to leave him to go to our lots. Considering that she was his favorite sister, her answer somewhat surprised me. She said she hoped he was not dreaming his time away, as he had done in London. Was nearly smothered by smoke last night, by the falling of the damper. Next day did not go to church, but read the Witness and Chambers Magazine. Sold Jonathan G. a few cords of dry wood at seventy-five cents a cord, drew several cords of dry and green wood to Aston village during the week; a cord of green wood is ample load for an average team of horses, and the roads must be good at that. In the latter part of the week drew bark, average load, one cord and twenty feet. It greatly tires a man's patience when the roads are bad, sometimes part of the sleigh or harness will break, or the load upset where the road is one sided, which is enough to try any man's temper, especially in cold weather to stand for over an hour in the biting wind reloading the load. Went to church on Sunday. Mabel Willoughby has returned from an academy, for the Christmas holidays. I met Florence Meredith, she told me that her mother returned from Scotland this morning. Tom went to church on Christmas day and dined at Mr. Willoughby's. I dined at G's.; had roast beef, goose, plum pudding with sauce, potatoes, bread, tea, butter, and sugar. Went with my aunt Sarah, Jonathan, Walter and Ethel to Devlin's in the evening; they sang songs and told riddles till twelve o'clock. Returned home by one o'clock. I drew bark and wood the rest of the week. For some loads I got from six to seven dollars. Tried to sell Mr. Meredith wood, but found that he had his supply. Uncle Richard and Clifford arrived from Montreal on the twenty-ninth, they drove out with horse and sleigh, they stayed at G's. I could not take a load to Aston next morning as it had snowed nearly two feet during the night. Chelton paid me twenty in gold for bark I had drawn to him in the afternoon; I went to Aston with uncle Richard and Herbert, who went to inquire about the strike of the railroad men on the Great Central Railway. We spent New Year's eve at G's. On New Years we visited our neighbors which we have not omitted to do since we were little children; then we used to try who could pay the visit the earliest, sometimes paying the visit as early as four o'clock. a. m. Mrs. C. treated us to candy, plum cake and tea. Uncle and Clifford, returned to Montreal in the afternoon, set the sawing machine, and put logs in a rollaway, ready for sawing but there was too much snow to get at the logs, so we gave up the idea, and will have to chop our stove wood.

FRAGMENTARY VERSES.

Who is it that sees a summer breeze,
A rustling in the branches of the trees,
And the feathered songsters on high
Warbling forth their happiest melody.

And the brilliant sun sending down
Its warmth and heat,
To make the earth produce replete
All that's required for man and beast:

And the same heat doth lift from Ocean bed
The waters there by rivers led,
And in a light and vapory form
Are carried o'er earth by summer's storm,
And on fields of shining grain
Are made discharge by atmospheric change
And doubts whether this is all by chance
Or by a Being great and divine created.

Who is there on board a ship
Baffled by the the approaching storm,
That sees the masts all torn and split
By the fury of the storm,
And sees the decks all rent and torn
By lightning's vivid force,
And hears the captain's trembling cry
My men we are all lost.
And amidst the groans,
And shrieks and moans,
Cry out there is no God.

Many there are who in this world live,
Who enjoy all the pleasures that it can give,
But never give a thought or a care
About the next world or for it prepare.
Some there are who waste their time,
Whose greatest gods are garments fine;
Of naught they think but their own self,
And how to spend their enormous wealth
Of which they never earn a dollar,
For they no trade or profession follow;
Good they are to stroll the streets
And with gay friends, costly dinners eat,
Or float about in the giddy dance,
And try some fair one to entrance
With their stylish dashing ways,
They sometimes win one by a chance
A flirt, a giddy one, a gay,
Who like themselves, are of no use
But waste their time in a useless way.

The wind was bleak,
The rain was cold;
The trees and branches creaked,
And some there fell that were too old
As the storm against them beat.

While in Montreal I visited Joe Beef's, place, a saloonkeeper who has acquired much notoriety from his eccentricity. The floor is strewn with sawdust; the whole house has a dark and gloomy appearance, with all sorts of rubbish scattered about in every direction. Close behind the bar was a human skeleton, which had a horrible appearance. The parlor has a piano in it, and is free to all temperance lecturers and preachers to hold their meetings in. He is very liberal to the poor, and has slices of beef and bread on the counter at the bar to give away to the poor who frequent his saloon. But all this is to attract custom, as are also the bears and deer he keeps. While in the bar-room a man dropped down as if dead, striking his head with fearful violence against a post. Joe Beef came quickly from behind the bar armed with a drunkard's restoratives, namely: red pepper and vinegar, which he rubbed with brutal violence over the poor man's face. The poor wretch writhed, groaned and ground his teeth. I never saw a face so haggard or marked with such hopeless despair; it was a sight that would have more influence on a man than a dozen temperance lectures. In the dining room the woman that waited on the table had the appearance as if she had melted blubber on a whaling ship for the last half century without changing her clothes—men must truly not be very fastidious to eat in such a place. And it is an outrage on the Christianity and civilization of any Christian nation to allow such places to exist openly in their midst.

In the evening I met the inebriate at Boneventure railway station and related to him the scene in the morning. He showed no shame; he appeared to be too far gone for that, and replied:

"Yes, stranger, I took too much for my good this morning, but I must have drink, I cannot live without it. Please lend me twenty-five cents, which I will return when I arrive at Troy, New York, where I reside.'

I replied that I would no more think of lending him money to buy whisky with than I would to buy arsenic; for both articles are much abused and used by men as a means of self-destruction. "Can't you see that this cursed drink will destroy you body and soul. However, before the train leaves, we will have time to take some supper."

After supper he asked for "just enough to buy one glass with." I grew indignant and said:

"Don't you see you are fast sinking into a pitiable and desperate condition. Be a man. It is not too late yet to save yourself from ruin and misery. You have brains and intelligence—use them for the purpose God gave them to you for. Be noble and courageous and resist and destroy this burning desire for drink. Never let yourself be seen again in the despicable condition you were seen this morning. Resolve from this time forth to cast off forever the shackles of the slavery of drink. Do not stay over night in Montreal; leave for Troy by the next train. You say you have friends there; go there to them and state your case; they will not refuse you their assistance. Keep even from the sight of drink. Have some fixed aim or object in view; concentrate on this object all your energy and talents. You will find that this will give you an interest in life and divert your thoughts from drink. And always keep before you that the noblest and grandest heroes are those who conquer themselves and rise from the lowest depths and become useful and honorable members of society."

That silken thread does stronger grow,
It fills his heart with bitter woe.
Why to that treacherous pleasure did he bow,
That holds his soul in bondage now.
At first 'twas pleasing to the eye,
But with such pleasures dangers lie
And if on man it once has power,
Is to that man a fatal hour.
Its cruel meshes he ne'er can break
Eternal misery is his fate.
His noble thoughts are by it crushed,
The voice of conscience by it hushed
And all that is noble bows to the dust.
He is as iron covered with rust
It marks his goodly brow with shame,
No longer honored is his name.
His face though once 'twas bright and fair
Is marked by its corroding care.

Resolutions each day he does make,
And the day after does them break.
Shall he for its deceitful pleasure
Lose honor, friends? No he shall never.
He'll crush the demons from his heart
And from its guilty pleasures part.
But alas, ere a few weeks pass away
In the mire deeper does he lay.
His heart is then filled with despair
His life's mistake he cannot repair.
Man's heart was filled with such anguish
As in despair he then does languish;
Death he would with pleasure greet
If his Creator he had not to meet;
Too wicked he is to die,
Too wretched for to live,
This is the way that sin rewards
Those who in her pleasures live.

A TEETOTALER'S VIEW OF THE LIQUOR QUESTION.

From the wheatfield there now came a rattling sound.
Farmer Jones with his reaper at work I found.
He said wheat this year will not pay,
But I am in luck, I am glad to say
For I sold my wheat three weeks ago
Before the price went down so low.
'Twas to the brewer Mr. B.
A barrel of ale he gave me free.
I said I am sorry you sold your wheat
To such a miserable cheat;
For most of the beggars in the town of C.,
Are caused by this same Mr. B.
Many begin with his fine stout ale
And end their days in common jail;
Many who drank his fine old rye
In drunkard's graves dishonored lie.

Not satisfied with his deadly sport,
Light foreign wines he must import,
With which to coax the novice in,
Then a reeling drunkard make of him.
I once remember the town of C.,
From strong drink's curse 'twas almost free.
But now on almost every street
His saloons and victims you may meet;
Some with their fine gold lettered sign
Where gentlemen may pass their time.
And in its parlors cool and nice,
There sip their liquors cooled in ice.
More harm these do than all the rest.
For here it is no drunkard's nest;
'Tis merely a preparing place
Drunkards to make of the coming race.
What a very kind man is Mr. B.,
With all young men he is so free;

A billiard table he expressly bought,
Of young men's pleasure, he only thought.
It would be so nice of a rainy day
To meet together and at billiards play.
Alas how oft with winning smile,
He thus does fine young men beguile
To take a light drink at his bar,
Or smoke with him a choice cigar.
He slippery arguments does prepare,
As innocent youths he does ensnare.
Young gents, he oft to them would say
I have been a drinker for many a day
Now liquor with benefit a man may use,
But he its good should not abuse.
A great many people of this place
Abuse me almost to my face,
And say I am going to ruin their son
Because I give him a little fun.
Now I don't like to see a young man wild,
But he should not be ruled as a little child;
Gents, I'll tell you the truth, and to say the least,
Some men have appetites worse than a beast;
Now such men as these I do abhor,
May they never enter my bar room door.
A man who cannot himself control
Does not deserve man's name to own,
But these temperance fanatics always cry,
Those who touch liquor will surely die.
Just look at Squire Jones
He has never passed the temperate zones;
Altho' he has drank for many a year,
His wife never shed for him a tear.
A better father or husband cannot be found,
Or a man with better judgment sound;
He is a member of our church, I say
And in church almost every Sabbath day
He is the best farmer in the place,
No crops or time by him waste
And he has thousands in the bank,
Altho' twenty years he has drank.
Come! Come! cries Harry Hall,
We'll drink a bumper, one and all
To the great and jolly Squire Jones,
Who never passed the temperate zones.
Then Mr. B., with smile most bland,
To them the poisoned cup did hand.
'Twas not vile whisky they drank there,
As some poor man bound by drink's snare;
'Twas sparkling transparent champagne,
That quickened the blood of many a vein.
As I these words had said,
His face with anger had flushed red,
He quickly caught me by the arm
No joke from a man raised on a farm;
His grip 'twas like an iron vice,
I felt it far from being nice.
He in a voice of thunder spoke,
Which in me sleeping terrors woke.
Said make to me an apology now
Or I'll throw you in yonder slough,
Mr. Jones, I unto him did say,
Beg pardon if I have offended in any way,
No insult I ever meant to you,
I only said what was too true;
But before on this subject we further speak,
Allow me to inform you that my arm is weak

And that your most affectionate grasp,
You'll now have the kindness to unclasp,
For the very marrow in my arm's bone
Does your arm's zeal and fervor own.
My hand by friends was often clasped
With friendship's pressure firm,
But I ne'er yet got such grasp
As from your friendship stern;
But as my arm is now released,
I will to you explain
A subject which to say the least
Will cause us both great pain:
'Twas yesterday about midday,
I walked through the town of C.,
And there I met poor William J.,
As drunk, as drunk could be.
He was a handsome fellow once
His mother's pride and hope
But cursed drink that beauty took;
'Tis now a horrid sight,
His eyes they are all bleared,
His face 'tis nearly red,
By him his God no longer feared,
And conscience voice just dead.
Along the streets he reeling went
Singing a drunken air,
His aged mother with grief bent,
At the doorway met him there;
I'll ne'er forget that look of woe
On that poor mother's face,
As towards her, her only son did go
With a drunken staggering pace.
His face, poor fellow, it grew sad,
As he gazed on his mother's face.
Still in his heart, he some good had,
Which drink had not effaced,
But ere he could her pardon ask,
She a cry of anguish gave
And sank upon the dark green grass,
Lost to all that ever she had loved
On this side of the grave.
Poor J., to his senses quickly came,
And o'er his mother wept;
Feelings there now o'er his heart came,
Which long before had slept.
But even suppose he does reform,
And break the demon's power,
His mother he never can restore,
Or childhood's pure lost hour.
He once the blessing had of health,
But now has it no longer,
Drink took both it and all his wealth,
We on this case may ponder;
I regret calling Mr. B., a cheat
But still you cannot wonder
For cases like this we often meet,
Of which he is the founder.
Now Mr. Jones I do not wish to be rude,
Or in your affairs myself intrude,
But I want your influence which is great,
And in the town of C., has considerable weight.
To crush from it drink's fearful vice,
And close those fine cool barrooms nice,
Also these low vile haunts of sin,
Where the drunkard staggers for his gin;
And sometimes pawns his poor wife's cloak,

8

For brandy wherewith himself to soak;
He his poor wife and children in misery leaves,
They only blows and cuffs from him receive,
How frightful is a drunkard's end,
As with contortions he does bend.
His room is filled with fearful shrieks,
As with gleaming eyes he round it leaps,
He suffers from delirium tremens,
The room to him is full of demons.
Oh! what a frightful death is this!

Can this man e'er see heaven's bliss?
We all know the words the Bible says,
Enter heaven a drunkard never may.
A fearful crime is it not then
Drunkards to make our fellow men.
A felon's crime can be no worse,
Of man he only kills the first,
But he that his neighbor with drink fills,
Does soul and body by it kill.

A MODERATE DRINKER'S VIEW OF THE LIQUOR QUESTION.

In my opinion the evils from the use of spirituous liquors are greatly exaggerated. Some over zealous prohibitionists assert that over two-thirds of the crime of this country is caused by the use of spirituous liquors. This estimate is utterly incorrect, as any one can see who reads the records of crime in the daily papers, and places against each cause its just amount of crime. Liquor is by many unjustly charged with crimes that are the fruits of ignorance, superstition and those evil passions that some men allow to gain a supremacy in their hearts. If wicked men take their own lives or the lives of their fellow men by the use of poison, would it be wise or right to deprive the rest of mankind of the benefits derived from its proper use, even though it was a source of destruction to thousands of depraved men? The poison is not the real cause of all the suicides by it in the world. It comes from many other causes—the chief cause being a want of education and moral training in childhood. Everything that has been made is for man's use: he, as lord of creation, must be taught to maintain his supremacy over all things and not to act in a cowardly manner, throwing away the gifts of God and man's invention because a few of his fellow men abuse them, and bring ruin on themselves. Are we to deprive ourselves of the benefits of commerce because millions of men and money have been lost and swallowed up by the oceans of this earth? By no means. We will with patience and ingenuity conquer the perils of the deep and make all things become subservient to the wants and pleasures of mankind. Some extremists may advocate an almost primeval simplicity in dress and diet, and say that costly dress, food and liquors are not necessary for life. This to a certain extent is true, but when they assert that millions of money are wasted annually on costly liquors, men of moderation deny the statement and treat it with ridicule. Man can live on the plainest and coarsest of food, but why should he? If an Almighty Creator ordained that man should live on and use only what was absolutely necessary for his existence, He would never have created some of the most beautiful flowers, which are only useful inasmuch as they gratify the senses of smell and sight. What a dreary and monotonous world this would be if all the people were foolish enough to adopt the almost Spartan simplicity that some people advocate. Man would become merely a machine for accumulating wealth, and the greatest part of the elegant, delicious and costly luxuries that now exist would vanish from the face of the earth, and with them the punch bowl and wine glass, no longer to be used as a delightful, exhilarating solace after fatigue and exposure to cold rainfalls of autumn or the piercing winds of winter. What nonsense! We will not deprive our sense of taste of its greatest enjoyment because a few men make beasts of themselves. Let laws be made to make all men respect the dignity and honor of their manhood, and oblige them to do so. A certain amount of freedom must be allowed all men in countries that boast of political and religious liberty— in fact, perfect liberty ought to be given all men in everything that does not injure their fellow men or retard the progress of civilization. But when a man unfits himself for the citizenship of the nation, by committing slow suicide, and half starves and ill-treats his family, he should be looked upon as a public malefactor and punished accordingly by the government of his country. Prohibitionists bring this small ignoble class of men before the public as a proof of the necessity of prohibition, keeping in the background thousands of the noblest, wisest and cleverest men that have existed, and do exist, who have used and enjoyed spirituous liquors in all their forms and died at a good old age in no way lamenting or regretting their use of them. I am of the opinion that our legislators ought not to prohibit anything that exists, whether in its natural state or invented by men, that adds to man's pleasure and comfort even if some men do abuse those gifts and bring ruin on themselves, but legislate against their abuse and not against their use. If prohibition ever becomes a necessity and the government has to adopt it through the force of public opinion, it will be an eternal disgrace to the people of this nation and put their civilization to shame, placing them in a somewhat similar position to the naughty child whose parents have to lock the sweetmeats out of its way to keep it from childish excess and sickness. Man's civilization it is true is not yet complete, but surely if the savage beast of the forest through instinct can avoid poison and gluttony, man with his grand and mighty intellect can be so educated and civilized that he will in future years no longer give way to those excesses that cause so much ruin and misery on the earth. Just and severe laws should be made against men and women who in any way whatever retard the physical and mental development of the human race.

A day 'tis very short,
Yet still in it do thousands die
Their pardons yet unsought;
Thousands are born in a day,
Through life they have yet to go.
Some of them good men make,
Others by sin cast low;
Till our prisons and our jails
Through their deeds of crime,
Many an awful end attain
In reward for their life time.

Many begin with splendid hopes,
Have all they can desire,
And end their days with a hangman's rope.
With their souls in peril of eternal fire.
Others love this world so much
They think not of the next;
They have no sins to make them blush,
Their conscience is at rest.
To church they go on the Sabbath day,
They lead a holy life.
With sinners class us not, they say,
We lead a better life.
They say the Bible is God's word,
Its precepts true and just,
Salvation it to all affords,

Who in its promises trust;
But if they have a neighbor,
That is not of their class,
Who lives by honest labor,
On the street they will him pass;
And within their elegant drawing rooms bright.
For hours they will talk with one of their set,
On business and fashions,
Whether this or that's right.
For mere baubles of fashion,
Their very souls fret.
Sometimes they give a dollar or so,
To spread the gospel's light;
Then the very next day to a jeweler's go
And spend thousands on a tiny gem bright.
Most of their precious time they spend
In dancing and silly games.
Did God for this on earth man send,
With his intelligent brains?
What a shame rich men to see
Spend thousands on a trifling gem,
When deserts untilled lie from sea to sea
And in ignorance perish his fellow men.

The day is dark and cloudy
Dark mists hang o'er the sky,

The hay has shot already,
And is nearly two feet high.
The storm of yesterday evening,
All nature had refreshed.
The crop grew while men were sleeping,
In their beds at rest.
Many people are passing,
Going to Aston market,
Some of produce have a load
Others of eggs a basket,
But many to the village go
Merely to pass the day.
Liquor like water does then flow,
Down the throats of Frenchmen gay.

'Twas on a balmy evening,
In the pleasent month of June.
I through the leafy forest walked.
By the pale light of the moon.
Amidst the trees the lights flicker,
In shadows here and there,
And in some places where the leaves were
    thicker,
Darkness complete reigned there.
All nature was silent and tranquil,
'Twas nearly as silent as death,
Save the distant cry of a whippoorwill,
And the rustle of leaves by air's gentle breath.

The nineteenth century how advanced,
Beyond the savage age that's past.
Each nation's power is nicely balanced
The reins of government by statesmen grasped
Who for practical knowledge and sense,
By mortal man were ne'er surpassed;
They all now see 'tis common sense
Instead of wit and eloquence.
That makes a nation last.
No longer fops and spendthrifts
Stand around our country's throne.
'Tis men endued with nobler gifts.
Under which our country has grown.
Till now it ranks throughout the earth,
Midst nations, great and small,
As the land where liberty had its birth,
Where tyrants surely fall.
'Twas here the slave was first set free
From bondage, worse than death,
'Twas from the monarch of the sea.
That tyrany met its death.
Safe in this favored land
Surrounded by the wave,
Fine noble men from other lands
Come here their lives to save.
Who lack the monarch and the laws,
With which our country's blessed.
Because they tried to change their laws,
Their monarchs threatened death.
They in a cruel despotic way,
O'er their poor subjects rule.
Till their indignant subjects cry
Why let this tyrant rule?
Then led by desperate leaders,
Nought can arrest their zeal;
They are truly national weeders
The nation their cruelties feels.

But they once having tasted liberty,
Forget that even it has an end;
And from their tall poles of liberty,
To the guillotine noblemen send.
Some of these deserved their fate
For their deeds of tyrannical crime,
Others deserve a better fate
In reward for their life time.
Thus through the fault of a monarch,
Much innocent blood was shed,
Through his not having courage and firmness,
He at the guillotine lost his head.
Each day their frenzy grew greater.
Till their brutality knew no bounds;
Innocent blood did flow as water,
Throughout their principal towns,
Till all people of moderation
Were disgusted with their deeds,
And there came a great reaction,
When Napoleon his country freed.
At first they made him consul,
But his ambition craved for more,
And he higher grew in the national council,
After each victorious war,
Till the people were dazzled with glory
Won by their general brave;
And forgot about tyranny formerly,
To him the reins of government gave;
Thus the nation's mighty effort
In liberty's noble cause,
Did now become of no effect.
And was lost amidst the applause
Which they rendered to their Emperor,
As he returning came.
Of homage they could not give enough
To his great, glorious name,
Had our colony, when it rebelled
On American's distant shore,
The bounds of propriety levelled,
They ne'er would have gained the war.
But their acting with moderation,
And our distance from the scene,
Caused them to become a nation,
Which for one hundred years they have been.
For the loss of such a colony,
The British subjects all lament,
Especially the trifling cause,
Which caused her to absent
From her dutiful allegiance
To the land that gave her birth;
'Twas by our statesmen's negligence,
The war began at first,
They tried to tax unjustly,
The colonists would not submit.
Our foolish statesmen would not give way;
Thus the flames of war were lit,
But even then there yet was hope
To save England's fairest daughter;
But our statesmen would not stoop,
With foreign troops they fought her.
After many fierce battles, we were defeated,
'Twas what our country deserved,
And from America our soldiers
Then quickly retreated,
Which unto this day we might have preserved
If our statesmen had not.

Been so foolishly stubborn
And yielded to them,
In whatever was right.
Most of America
To them would have yielded,
And we never would have had
That inglorious fight;
But now it is too late
To amend the deeds of the past,
Our colony is now a power first rate.
Each year 'tis increasing so fast,
That in a few years it will pass us.
As a great manufacturing power,
They already surpass us,
In gold's heavy dust
And the exportation of flour.
With England they rank throughout the
　　world;
For intelligence and wealth
Like England, where e'er their flag's unfurled
Its influence is felt;
No longer the common masses
In ignorance remains,
And hear nothing but high and low classes,
As in devout priest ridden Spain.
Reader if e'er you travel,
Through the wide, wide world.
Mark well the difference between those coun-
　　tries,
Where liberty's flag is unfurled,
And those where ignorance and superstition,
And the power of priests remains.
As in Italy, Mexico and Spain.
Compare them with Great Britain,
Or countries of its race,
Or with Prussia, Holland, Denmark,
Can you a difference trace?
Yes, you cannot deny it,
The difference is great.
Go travel through sunny Italy,
Walk through the streets of Rome.
Return to England's temperate clime,
Gaze from St. Paul's church dome,

I do not the difference over state,
When I say the change is great,
As daylight is unto darkness,
Or as life is unto death,
Yet Italy has a lovely clime,
As ever was stirred by air's gentle breath,
'Twas once the fairest of countries,
With a people both noble and brave,
Their territory scarce knew a boundary.
Save the ocean's restless wave;
Their senators knew naught of dishonor,
'Twas modesty adorned their maids
'Twas patriotism sent their youth unto battle
And by virtue they lengthened old age,
When they conquered all nations of size,
Throughout the then known earth;
Virtue by them was less prized,
And they spent all their time in mirth,
'Twas the loss of virtue.
With pleasure and wine,
That made the greatest nation,
Of this our earth decline.
Through ages have passed
Since a nation they have been.
Grand works of their creation,
Throughout the land are seen.
Why now does Italy and Rome,
Once the mistress of the world,
With its palaces of stone,
In such misery abound?
Why does ignorance and vice,
This glorious land disgrace,
When Christ's most holy Vicar,
Here dictates to our race?
Bulls and dogmas issue from him,
To over half the Christian world,
While Rome itself is full of sin,
To the whole world a disgrace,
With its convents and churches,
On almost every street,
While every second man you meet,
Is either a monk or priest.

TO A FRIEND WHO ASSERTS THAT WAR IS A DREADFUL NECESSITY.

Cities are burnt,
The harvests are spoiled,
And nation's wealth wasted,
By wars turmoil;
Religion forbids its gastly strife,
This alone should cause those nations to
　　cease,
That have received the gospel's light
And from stern war give them relief,
For we have no cause to yet complain
On our earth for want of space.
For untilled lands lie from sea to sea,
A large and trackless waste,
On our little globe we still have space,
For millions more of men.
Why then not wait some thousand years,
Till 'tis filled from end to end,
And leave to our great Creator,
The problem of finding space.

On our earth in coming years
For the increase of our race
Though our age is far advanced,
Beyond the savage age that's past,
We still can more improvements make,
And further still advance,
Towards the glorious age that's coming,
When all the world will be at peace.
When virtue and wisdom,
Will reign supreme
O'er ignorance and vile deceit.

'Twas on a Sunday bright and fair,
To Richford river with a friend I went;
Clouds edged with silver decked the air.
That to the sky a beauty lent;
After a drive of about three miles,
Over a road that was none too smooth.
We at the Rousseau farm arrived,

'Twas a sight fit for a poet's muse
With its gentle rising grass-covered slopes,
Its tall and stately elms
The crops that were the farmer's hopes,
Which in the breezes trembled,
The dark green oats, the lighter wheat,
The well kept kitchen garden,
The potatoes in their rows so neat,
The neat and tidy barn,
Of which no boards were lying loose
Nor doors from off their hinges,
But everything neat in its place
From the ground floor to the shingles,
The dark, broad, silent river
With a current that scarcely moved
Its winding course through meadows
Till it to the mill dam flowed;

This mill it had a rustic look
With its rough moss-covered posts.
'Tis years since work its timbers shook,
Or boards were from it tossed,
It now stands but an emblem,
Of what it was that day,
When in the morning its men assembled,
'Twas then activity;
But now its timbers are decayed,
The machinery from it gone.
'Tis a lonely place in evening's shade;
Its mill dam is half gone,
The waters having forced their way
Through planks no longer sound,
Rush against the rocks,
Rise high in spray,
And down the rapids bound.

IN REFERENCE TO CANADIAN FARMERS.

Our farmers want ambition,
With the times they keep not pace.
Some think that education
For a farmer is a waste;
That strength is all he needs
With which to till his land;
But he that lacks bright intelligence,
Can never expect to stand
High midst his fellow-men of worth,
Whose society is a pleasure.
Education of all things is the first,
By which to reach their level.
How often of an evening
They might their minds improve,
By study and constant reading,
But precious time they lose,
Some often sit at twilight,
And have their evening's smoke,
Every half hour filling their pipes,

And puff them off in smoke.
If the money they spent on drink and tobacco,
Which on an average amounts to fifty dollar,
 a year,
Was spent on good books
Full of practical knowledge,
What a different class they then would
 appear.
Not as they are at the present day.
With other professions they cannot compare.
In literature and politics,
They have scarce naught to say,
And in their country's affairs,
They have no equal share;
But this will soon be a thing of the past,
Their education has already begun,
No longer they will be an ignorant class,
For the father now educates his son.

[Written after a fight I witnessed between two French Canadian brothers, many of whom have the beastly habit of biting their antagonist when he is getting the best of them: fingers or the ears are considered the most advantageous parts to bite. I have personally known one man who had one of his fingers disabled in this way.]

Romulus and Remus,
Two men of great renown.
One of them forever famous
Having built Rome's ancient town,
One day did have a quarrel.
And against each other went,
The eldest brother's hand was soiled,
He his brother's life's blood shed.
'Twas many many years since then,
In this enlightened age,
Two only brothers against each other,
Did in fierce combat wage.
Their hearts were filled with dreadful ire,
Their eyes flash with anger's fire,
'Twas a sad and cruel sight
As there they fought by the pale moon's
 light,

One of them like a cruel beast,
Caught his brother by the shoulder,
And in it sank his snow white teeth
Till his poor brother hollered.

"Imperial Cæsar, dead and turned to clay,
Might stop a hole to keep the wind away."
'Twas Shakespeare who wrote these lines,
I will not dispute their truth,
But from Cæsar's death to our present time,
Has honor his name forsook?
No never! and unto this day,
Even yet in ages to come,
Honored shall be his name
For the deeds which his valor have done;
For the heart that never quailed before
 danger,
That mourned an enemy's death;

In whom all fear was a stranger.
By his heroic and tragic death,
He has won everlasting fame.
Throughout the civilized earth.
Republicans and Monarchies may vanish
    away,
But never his name from this earth,
The youths as yet unborn,
With ages that are yet to come,
With interest, will read the story,
Of how he fought and won.
May it give their hearts ambition.
When they hear of his success,
May it stir them to activity,
Send them in honor's quest.
For in seeking their own honor.
In a just and lawful way,
Their country's honor is advanced,
Just as much as they.

We worked beside the leafy forest,
Through which the moonbeams struggled
    through.
'Twas a lovely sight to gaze on,
The sky was naught but azure blue,
There was not a cloud on the vaulted heavens.
From the north to the south not one could be
    seen.
For a moment here and there a star's light
    did glimmer.
The next moment a blank where the star had
    been,
But ere one short half hour had passed
Millions of stars lit up the sky,
Quickly through space bright meteors
    flashed
And vanished in a moment's time.

Where is there a man, in country or town,
At the end of the day's toil
Whose heart will not grow light
As enters his happy home
Does hear the kettle's cheerful boil.
His children his steps have known,
Around him they flock lovingly
And take his tools away;
His wife has a loving look;
His weariness flies away.

There is work for every man
Whose motto is duty done
Throughout this great Canadian land
E'en for every Adam's son.
Let our rulers rule with wisdom
This great Canadian land
And never try to loosen
The ties that bind our land
With our mother country
Across the ocean's wave,
But rather try and strengthen them
Till one great nation is made
Of England and her colonies
On which the sun never sets.
By this we would stronger be,
For our strength would us protect,
And we could then make a stand

Midst the nations of the earth.
And banish war from off our land,
Which often in it has caused death.
Yet should some other nation
With us injustice treat
And armies send out against us,
We then should not retreat,
But, as one united nation,
Against them make a stand
And those unjust invaders
Drive from our native land.

By yonder woodlands across the stream
Hundreds of fireflies are there
For a moment a thousand lights are seen
Then empty darkness fills the air.

The woodlands no longer
Look bare and dreary
Without their coat of verdure green
On them each day leaves are appearing
And violets at their trunks are seen.

The mosquitos, what a nuisance
To the human race!
Gentle ladies lose their patience,
Tear their lovely hands and face
Till one is almost afraid
That their beauty they will lose
If they they thus continue on
Their beauty to abuse.
With what pretty indignation
A lady brings her tapering hand
With an energetic slap
Where the stinging insect stands:
She smiles a smile of pleasure
When she kills the "little wretch."
But a hundred come from the neighboring
    swamp
To avenge their comrade's death.
She tries to read a book,
On her favorite rustic seat,
But ere she has read a single line
Her rout it is complete.
She toward the house goes
With a light and hasty step.
There is even a frown on her once even
    brow.
At the gate she has John met,
Tells him to go and light a smudge
By yonder elm tree,
She thinks she can bear with nasty smoke
If from mosquitoes she can be free.
John lights a smudge with the greatest care
Does green leaves on it lay--
Columns of smoke mount through the air—
She thinks she has won the day,
Goes sits upon her rustic seat
With interest reads her book;
But the wind has changed another way
And envelops both her and book
With clouds of suffocating smoke.
Her eyes are filled with tears--
She cries this would a saint provoke.
Her favorite seat she leaves.
If she to the barnyard had gone

She there would have easily seen
That the animal world as well as man
The stings of mosquitoes feel—
Here the spirited horse goes prancing round
In a wild and frantic way,
But at the sound of his master's voice
Welcomes him with a gladsome neigh—
The farmer makes a good-sized smudge,
The moment the smoke appears
The animals all around it crowd,
For smoke they have no tears,
And if they did it were for joy
For the comfort they receive ;
For the flies no longer bother them
Or sting them in the ears;
No longer is dignity known—
To get an equal amount of smoke
All most together meet,
The horses and cows, the calves and the
  sheep,
With the colts and the lambs
With their frolics and freaks
Till the break of the next day.
The impatient cow will hardly stand
To let the maid her milk
And sometimes with a kick
Upsets the can with the evening's milk
Or brings her tail with sudden force
Against the maiden's face:
Its bright fresh color it has lost,
It on it leaves a trace
Which will require both soap and water
Once more her to restore
To be the farmer's pretty daughter
That she had been before.
But it is our sturdy lumbermen
Who work in the forest's gloom
That know what pests the mosquitoes are
While they take their dinner at noon;
To make a smudge they run a risk
Of a general conflagration,
For the ground everywhere is dry and crisp,
And they know what desolation
A forest fire causes
As it rushes up the trees,
And that it scarcely ever pauses
Till it nought of value leaves;
They, therefore, do not light a smudge
As they take their noon day meal.
They hear the mosquito's constant buzz
And their stings they often feel.

How bright and frosty the morning,
The snow flakes hang upon the trees,
'Tis a silver forest as the sun is dawning,
It nigh surpasses Summer leaves.

The sun has just risen in a tinted sky
And the flowers no longer drooping lie,
For, beneath its bright and genial heat,
Unfolded their beauties are complete,
The gentle breezes blow the air
In its sweetest fragrance everywhere,
The feathered songsters welcome day
With their happiest melody,
All creation seems refreshed

After a tranquil night of rest.
When all creation seems so bright
No man should have but a heart light,
Excepting those that trouble know
Or in sin's guilty pathway go.
'Twas on a morning fair like this
O'er mountain top hung golden mist,
Still on the grass the dewdrops clung
As diamonds glittering in the sun,
I through the country took a stroll,
Watched the lambs frisk on grassy knoll,
Saw the young colts with coats so sleek
Gallop and o'er the ditches leap,
Heard their wise mothers' reproving neigh
For going so far from them away;
Saw a young calf too young to share
In its playmates' frolics there
With its comic wondering gaze
On this new world of a few days;
Also a hen with all her chicks
With all their cunning little tricks,
When one a grasshopper had caught
The others all around it popped
And seized its head, its wings and legs,
And all with relish on it feed—
The stately father with plumage gay
Is from them a few feet away,
A warning cry from him does come,
They towards their mother quickly run;
They in a mother's care confide
She with her wings does them all hide,
I soon saw the cause of the warning cry,
'Twas a chicken hawk soaring high up in
  the sky.
From these I turned another way:
There golden wheat the breezes sway,
Some thrifty man this wheat did sow,
But God alone could make it grow,
From Him the sun derives its heat
That makes the earth produce replete
All that's required for man's use,
Often put by man to sad abuse.
How can some foolish men declare
That on earth by chance came there?
Let them take a well tilled field
And try if produce it will yield
Kill all the seed that does in it lay
And from it keep all seed away.
If chance made this world here below
Something in that field by chance will grow;
But, no ! barren and bare it will remain
Year after year all the same.
If for one field chance can do naught
Can then a universe be wrought.
No ! None but God, the only Great,
Could this, our universe, create.

If there is an object of interest for men to
  see
'Tis a fine strong ship on a stormy sea,
But were it to lack a guiding hand
Seldom by chance it would safely land,
But driven by every changing storm
On rugged rocks it would be borne.
No man of sense would dare to say
That ship by chance on the sea lay.

But that some man that ship did build,
And with a cargo had it filled;
And to a crew its management gave.
Ere it went out on stormy wave;
Thus when Jehova the great and Divine,
The Ever Almighty, the Ruler of time,
Glanced o'er that dark and endless space,
Which then was naught but dreary waste,
Through his infinite power the Only Wise,
Our earth created as it now lies,
Also sun, moon and stars did make,
From which our universe
Its light doth take,
In this small corner of mighty space,
Our sun is the greatest;
Round it revolving all the rest go,
It heat and light doth on them throw,
Our sun immoveable does not stay,
Round larger suns its course does lay.
These suns with ours round larger go,
Father of space man may not know;
Of space man never can comprehend.
Of boundless space there is no end,

CATHOLICISM CRITICISED FROM A PROTESTANT STAND-POINT.

There is a God the only great,
That did the heavens and earth create.
Few men of reason do this deny.
Altho' portions of scripture they deny.
They admire some of its noble pages,
Others they look on as mere fables.
Of the superstitions Jewish nation,
With their ridiculous story of earth's creation
That God would delight in the blood of beasts,
Is a barbarous doctrine to say the least,
And worthy of the savage age
In which it was written in the sacred page.
Yet some Christian churches threaten with
hell.
All those who against their doctrines rebel.
And with the blasphemous imaginary threats
Have doubters and reasoners arguments met.
And for the last eighteen hundred years,
Have filled the world with doubts and fears,
And with their creed most base and wild,
Men must have faith as a little child,
For to exercise in religion intellect and reason,
Is accounted by them the rankest treason,
Mankind of course must have the faith of
babes,
To become for the priesthood suitable slaves,
Such as existed in the middle ages,
Which caused such a blot on history's pages;
'Twas the cruel bigotry of the church of Rome
That scattered o'er Europe the martyr's bones,
And made Galileo a man most learned,
Retract his statement that the world turned
round.
And with fire and sword laid waste
The peaceful valleys of the Albigense race,
And struck a medal to proclaim
Its pleasure in the thousands slain,
Of the brave Huguenots that would not
receive,
Or the errors of Rome believe.
It also blessed Philip the Cruel of Spain,
And encouraged him to try and reclaim
Germany and England from Luther's preach-
ing,
Which had almost dispelled the errors it was
teaching.
Was the sword and inquisition the proper
way
To lead back these lambs that had gone astray

And yet altho' guilty of all this infamy,
It proclaims from its pulpits its infallibility
And to-day is working with the vilest deceit,
To bring the world again in bondage at its
feet.
In Spain and Austria its bigotry still exists,
No man there can justice get who its tyranny
resists.
Not less than thirty reformers can meet to
worship,
Which in any age or country, is a great in-
justice,
And not many months ago,
Bible sellers received many a cruel blow
From the whips and clubs of Spanish priests,
Such treatment in America would not be,
given to a thief.
Yet some of their co-religionists,
That in Protestant countries live,
Take all they can,
But nothing give.
They enjoy the liberties of Protestant mag-
nanimity,
But in its glorious institutions, they have no
affinity,
They still believe their priest's malignant
lies.
And the glorious name of Luther despise,
And assert that the wonderful reformation,
Was but a disastrous revolution.
This revolution has taken place
In Germany, England and the United States.
Now I asked these Christians religiously
blind,
Where can they greater nations find,
In science, inventions and education,
They surpass all but the French nation,
Whose inhabitants rebelled against the
church's power,
And have been a greater nation since that
hour;
We need not, however, cross the ocean,
To see the effects of superstitious devotion.
In Brazil and Mexico what progress has been
made,
Since Spain to those countries the gospel
gave?
Truly it was a cruel sight. [gospel's light.
As the Spaniard with his sword spread the

9

How far more Christlike, was the heretic Penn.
For he treated the savages like fellow men,
And did not use such bloody treachery,
As the followers of the Roman Hierarchy
Yet the progress of the heretics has been grand,
While ignorance and superstition predominate
In every American Catholic land.
I challenge the most devout of the Catholic religion,
To prove otherwise, that their progress deserves derision,
When compared with the superior civilization
Of all the Protestant nations,
But I have often heard them reply in this way;
All the heretics' advantages perish on the judgment day.
Many of these religious dupes believe that penance and pain.
Is necessary to help them eternal life to gain.
Why should a man who abstains from meat,
Derive advantage from it at the judgment seat;
All that has been made is for man's use,
He only sins, who puts things to abuse.
Oh how the noble men of future ages,
Will deride the bloody penance of the middle ages,
And only by their noble actions please their God
Without the self chastisement of a monkish rod.
I have often felt mingled pity and contempt
When Catholic children have for an hour knelt,
Repeating a single prayer to God,
As a punishment in place of the chastening rod.
Oh, what a farce, to punish a child with prayer,
To have it love it should be the parent's care.
History proves that the greater faith of a nation,
The greater is its superstition and degradation:
Pagans and Mohammedans have a more unquestioning belief,
And have longer prayers and fasts
Than those who adore their God of bread at mass,
Yet their greater faith reduces their civilization
Below that of all the European nations.
Then again compare Roman Catholic people
With the Protestants that have a faith more feeble,
The Romanists believe with unquestioning deference
In anything to which their religion has reference,
And have a more childlike and unquestioning religion,
Or elevates and ennobles the human mind.

Than those who belong to Luther's great schism,
But by the fruits of their greater devotion,
Do they give the world any convincing token
That it makes them more noble and civilized nations,
Than those who their credulous faith have forsaken?
Ah, no! they cannot but are filled shame,
At their backwardness, for which their religion is to blame.
Rome for centuries governed by this infallible religion,
Is truly worthy of world's derision;
Situated in the fairest land of wine and flower
What was its progress under infallible power?
It lost its greatness of ancient day,
And only gained in gaudy church display;
With superstition and ignorance it became debased,
And as a first rate city and nation, lost its place;
But the scorn and contempt of the civilized world,
Roused dormant patriotism and the nation's flag unfurled,
Under which the Italians patriots brave,
To the country again, freedom and liberty gave.
Italy's progress since that time has been wonderful and great,
And again in Europe, it may become first rate,
Let us now compare London of the heretic school,
With Rome under the Pope's infallible rule,
Since London was reformed and Protestant became:
How great has been its increase in power, wealth and fame,
And also how much greater is its modern civilization,
Than that of any Catholic city or nation.
Excepting infidel Paris where the church's power is despised,
And in consequence it is the nation's pride.
What does holy Rome, or devout Madrid or Lisbon gain,
In the civilization they inferior remain,
Than the heretics and infidels who live far nobler lives,
And to a nobler and grander civilization rise.
But in American cities the homes of the brave
The heretics have still grander progress made.
Compare intellectual Boston, with any Brazilian city,
And it fills the hardest heart with pity
For the stagnant and ignorant Brazilian nation,
That is scarcely in a semi state of civilization.
And New York, the queen of American cities,
How much greater and grander than any Mexican city,
In everything that enriches and renders happy mankind,

Yet the Spaniards settled amongst superior
  nations,
Than the settlers of the Dutch or English
  nation.
They found a civilization that astonished the
  world
In Mexico and Peru that in riches did abound
And lands that had ten times more fertility
Than New England, noted for its sterility.
But oh, noble heretics' how great your civ-
  ilization,
Which is the admiration of every European
  nation;
While all the American nations of the Catho-
  lic religion
Are, through ignorance, in a deplorable con-
  dition.
Another proof of this church's debasing faith
Is seen in Lower Canada's semi-barbarous
  state.
Here are settled countrymen of the learned
  French nation,
In a pitiable state of degradation
Through the unrestrained spiritual power of
  priests,
From which the English have began to give
  them relief,
By the clear and convincing proof of their
  superiority.
Altho' in that province they are but a small
  minority.
It is English enterprise and their commercial
  activity,
That has created Canada's wealth and pros-
  perity.
This can be seen where English settlers live,
They to that town or village increased pros-
  perity give.
If any doubt this, to Montreal go,
And the English portion of it to them the
  truth would show.
Let them but see the beautiful English streets
Such as Sherbrook St., Catherine and Dor-
  chester St.,
And compare them with the miserable French
  architectural display,
And the difference is as great as darkness to
  day
Then again examine the names in every great
  work,
The names of the heretics always rank first;
But those places isolated from Protestant
  example,
Form a still more convincing sample
Of the terrible effects of unquestioning faith.
The curse of all nations in an ignorant state.
In these districts the schools mainly teach
The catechism and doctrines of the Catho-
  lic belief.
When these have been taught and their first
  communion taken,
Their education is finished and the school
  forsaken.
Thus in some parishes few can read or write.
But in its place the priests give them spiritual
  light,

And if on anything these slaves have a doubt,
Their spiritual advisers, for them the truth
  find out.
I have often seen thousands of these illiterate
  fools,
Become for the priesthood, political tools
And refuse their vote to an ex-Freemason,
Because he had once a secret oath taken;
Even though that society he now denounced,
And on bended knees its errors renounced,
And had a character without a stain.
These in the election were of no avail,
For his opponent was a tool of the priest,
And with a chosen few would often meet
At the house of their spiritual adviser,
The progress of the election to consider,
And on the Sunday preceding the election
  day,
The priest unto the people at the church did
  say:
I see the devil now in the church,
Encouraging the Liberals in their wicked
  work.
And when they die he will take them to hell
Because against our church they did rebel.
But for this tyrannical language this priest,
Through the indignation of the liberal press
  came to grief;
For all the liberal men throughout the prov
  ince
Sent to the bishop a wise remonstrance,
Against the power that this priest usurped,
And for aiding politicians in political work.
The consequence was he was sent away,
To another parish under ultramontane sway
For his political opinions and exhortations,
Would in such a parish cause no sensation,
But be received with unquestioning submis-
  sion.
Such was their ignorant and political con-
  dition,
That for thirty years they always elected
That man who for them their priest selected.
I have often conversed with men of this type
Where in a whole parish not twenty could
  write.
And asked them how they gained their opin-
  ion,
Before at the polls they gave their decision.
They answered that the speeches before the
  election
Gave them some light on the question.
"But we never come to a political decision,
Until we have had our confessor's opinion:
For how could any one but our spiritual ad-
  viser
Give us better advice, or make us wiser
In all that pertains to our race and religion,
The faithful should be guided by his decision
Thus the priests mostly favor the conserva-
  tive majority,
For it shows greater favors to the Roman
  hierarchy;
With laws that fill its coffers with gold,
And allows a French farmer's farm to be sold,
If he is unable his church tax to pay;

To gratify the priests in their church display
Millions of dollars on these churches are
wasted,
And for silly ceremonies they are conse-
crated,
Whereas if the money was spent on educa-
cation,
The Canadians would be a nobler nation,
If every church was turned into a school,
It would break the power of the priesthood's
rule,
And the people's manhood become more
elevated,
Though by secular education their churches
were desecrated.
The people would be taught to live nobler
lives,
And not the imagined beauties of a home in
the skies,
And not avoid sin on account of everlasting
punishment,
Or through the terrible fear of eternal judge-
ment;
But merely because a sinful and ignoble
life,
Destroys the happiness of human life.
But two incidents that among Romanists oc-
curred,
Have especially seemed to me sad and
absurd.

The first was not a dispute on spiritual be-
havior,
But a temporal one between a priest and his
neighbor,
Through which he did not his easter duties
fulfill;
And a short time after by accident was killed,
The priest refused to bury his in holy ground
And as none of his near relatives could be
found,
Some bigoted creatures of the church of
Rome,
Flung his body in a slough, and covered it
with stones,
Oh God of mercy, what horrid brutality
Was this base outrage on man's humanity!
The other incident occurred on Holy Friday;
That day in commemeration the Saviour
died on,
It was a statue of Christ that miraculously
bled,
At least so the people said,
But my cousin, who belonged to that church
Satisfied his curiosity and found out how it
worked,
'Twas sponges filled with the blood of ducks,
Which the priest's dupes imagined was mi-
raculous work.

My reason for criticising the Catholic church is because it, in my
opinion, is the greatest and most dangerous enemy of all the Christian
churches to religious liberty, liberal education and freedom of thought,
without which all the civilization and progress of the human race would
be stagnated, and man could never rise above the condition of semi-barbar-
ism. Protestantism has many errors, but there is a hope almost to a
certainty that they will be removed, for most of the Protestant churches
are liberal enough to keep up with the progress of civilization and remove
or modify doctrines that are repulsive to the more refined sentiments of
a more enlightened age. Not so with Romanism. It rigidly maintains
that all the doctrines it has taught, and does teach, are infallible, and by
horrible threats frightens men from using their reasoning powers on the
supernatural absurdities of their religion.

Now I ask all naturally liberal minded Catholics to study the history
of their church and carefully compare it with the remarkable progress of
civilization since the great and glorious light of Luther's reformation that
has spread throughout the earth.

To observing minds it is quite evident that most refined, educated
and prosperous Catholics are those that live in infidel and Protestant
countries, and that in all those countries where the population is almost
wholly Catholic, such as Lower Canada, Mexico, Peru, Chili and the
South American republics, the inhabitans are almost in a state of barbar-
ism when compared with the civilized, refined, educated people of the
American Protestant states, territories and countries.

Does it look possible that if the teachings of Catholicism were infallible and superior to those of Protestantism and infidelity that an all wise
God would allow the teachings of His Son's most holy vicar to have so

injurious effect on the childlike and unquestioning faith and lives of the
inhabitants of Spain, Austria, Poland, Portugal, Italy, Mexico, Chili,
Peru, Brazil and Lower Canada? Would He allow the lives of those who
have the firmest belief in this infallible religion to be in a more backward
and degraded state than the lives of heretics and infidels who live in Germany, France, England, the United States and other Protestant countries?
I think few men who reason impartially on the subject can think otherwise than this: That if Catholicism is the only true and perfect religion
on the earth that the majority of its believers should be the most perfect
and elevated people in existence.

History and the condition of the world at the present day utterly
refute all the pretensions of the Catholics being the most perfect people
in existence.

In Mexico and Peru the Spaniards repaid the generosity and hospitality of the natives with the basest treachery and bloodiest cruelty.
Their wars could not be called the wars of men, but the wars of devils.
The sword and cross went side by side; poor heathens were roasted to
death and so-called Christianity triumphed over paganism. And with
what effect? Go ask the travelers that stand amidst the ruins of
former greatness who see a people but a shadow of what they once
were, enslaved by priests and superstition, and they can give us the
answer. If this lamentable state of affairs only existed in one Catholic
country it might be attributed to some other cause, but it exists in all
countries where the church is all powerful.

I have lived many years among the French Canadians, and have never
met a people so destitute of all the delicacy of feeling and refinement. I
have seen over 1,100 people step up to the altar in three days' time
and partake of what they believed to be the body of God—a religious
rite that incurs fearful responsibilities on all Christians who partake
unworthily of it. Yet the majority of these people led low and worthless
lives and indulged regularly in swearing and indecent conversation.
What blasphemy is this, for a whole parish of drunkards, liars, lewd
men, thieves, backbiters, and many men and women who were merely
nominal Christians, as well as young children who could hardly realize
what they were doing, to all eat of the body of God, and then return in
half an hour's time to their old style of living. Just imagine the part of
the body of God going into a mouth that a few hours before took His
name in vain, uttered indecent jokes and anecdotes and stinking with
tobacco and bad whisky. I have often seen fathers and mothers talk in
their own homes before their innocent children in such a disgustingly
indecent manner that were such language used by any one in a respectable
English or American house he would certainly be kicked out by one of the
members of the family. English and Americans also use coarse language,
but the reader will no doubt have noticed that they almost invariably
respect the presence of the fair sex. Let it not be imaged that it is only
a few French families that are addicted to this habit. I have been in over
one hundred French villages and rural districts, and intimately associated
with many of the families, and have never meet one single family where
the men and boys wholly refrained from the use of oaths and indecent
language in the presence of their mothers, sisters and wives; and I have
never yet met a French woman who was not addicted to a mild form of

swearing and constantly using such exclamations of surprise as "Mon
Dieu, Seigneur de Dieu" etc. Yet, among these people, there are very
few who do not strictly observe all the holidays and fasts and regularly
confess and receive absolution. From conversations I have had with
them and many deaths I have seen amongst them, I am certain that
instead of gaining peace and consolation in time of death by a truthful
reliance on God's mercy and a purity and nobleness of action during life,
their only hope in time of death is based on two words—confession and
absolution.

I have often been disgusted at the cruel manner in which they galloped
their horses nearly to death get a priest with his little bit of bread, as if the
eternal happiness of an immortal soul could in any way be affected by
such a silly ceremony.

One of the most strange habits I saw among them was that of praying in the living room while all the other members of the family were
carrying on a lively conversation, and very often not of the choicest kind,
and intermingled with a few oaths. It certainly seemed very unchristian-
like conduct for people who were considered faithful and good members
of a perfect church, whose spiritual guide is claimed to be inspired by God,
but much more so, when the old man of 70 years of age, while on his
knees praying, cursed his son in a shocking manner for forgetting to bring
some things from the village, and then resumed his prayers and beads.
This, and hundreds of other things I shall relate later on, will go to show
that this religion is a mere formality and combination of silly rites and
ceremonies.

I have seen over fifteen hundred people going to the shrine of some
Saint, many of whom went to be cured of various diseases—but ot all
the fifteen hundred not one was cured. On asking the reason of this I
was told that those who went to be cured did not have sufficient faith.

This is the way with many religions of the present day—a plausible
statement is always found to defend that which does not deserve the name
of faith, but rather that of credulity. I could write of hundreds of
miracles that have been gravely related to me by the kind and hospitable
people on winter evenings, but for want of space will leave them for the
next volume. One of the most absurd, however, was that God had His
photograph taken on a "nose rag" from which all the pictures of the
present day of Him have been reproduced.

The woman of a house I boarded at had her child fearfully scalded,
and, for several days, applied nothing but holy water to heal it, but, as
any intelligent reader may imagine, without any beneficial result till even
the credulous mother gave way and she sent for a doctor.

It is perfectly sickening to see the unquestioning and childlike faith
they have in their priests to perform miracles—such as stopping fire and
floods or healing the sick, and actually one poor ignorant woman tried to
persuade me that a priest could raise a man from the dead—"that is if he
wanted to."

This of course is only in the isolated districts removed far from
the enlightening influences of Protestant freedom of thought. Many
perhaps who will read this will hardly believe that Catholicism isolated
from Protestantism and all powerful in a country tends to retard civilization and progress, and may point to the civilized condition of Catholics in

Protestant countries and countries under the influence of infidelity; but they should remember that no favorable conclusions can be taken for Catholicism from this fact; for, if that church does energetically support its schools in the United States, it is for the very reason that they are obliged to do so for fear their followers would attend national schools and become liberal minded citizens. Schools are also one of the best means they have in their power to impregnate the pliable minds of the rising generation with their doctrines.

I have no ill feelings against any individual Catholic or against the mass of the followers of that religion, but I must acknowledge I have a hearty contempt for those religious frauds who are secretly trying to undermine the institutions of this country and think of nothing else but the aggrandizement and augmentation of the power of their church by teaching doctrines directly antagonistic to the institutions of our country. I cannot tell how indignant I was, some time ago, when I read of the want of patriotism and base ingratitude of Archbishop Gibbon, of Baltimore, who actually had the audacity to use the following quotation: "Protestantism will perish and disappear as an ulcer with the last atom of flesh it has been cutting away." Oh, fellow citizens, just think of the base spirit that actuates the bigoted heart of this deceitful enemy of our country. He has the despicable meanness to wish the overthrow of the very institutions that gives him perfect religious liberty; that allows his church to buy some of the finest property in the country and build churches, schools and colleges on it. How grand does this liberal and generous treatment of our government to all the religious sects in the United States appear when compared with the mean and unjust treatment many of the Catholic governments give sects that are opposed to their religion. The sentiments of Archbishop Gibbon in the book entitled "The Faith of Our Fathers" only illustrates the policy of his tyrannical and ambitious church, which is to cry for rights and liberty when it is in the minority and crush to the earth all who are opposed to it when it is in the majority. But the idea, to call Protestantism an ulcer. If it is, no human tongue could utter a word vile enough for Romanism. It is not worth while, however, to waste time in speaking of a man who is so impregnated with bigotry that he cannot see the glorious work that Protestantism and its grand doctrines have accomplished in every country that had the blessing of its influence. Gibbon reminds me of the serpent who stung the foolish countryman that allowed it to warm itself at his fire-place. All such men as Gibbon are as dangerous to the nation as the serpent to the countryman, and it is absolutely necessary that our government should take the sting out of Catholicism and all other religions by taking completely out of their hands the education of the youth of the country. A government that gives all its citizens a liberal national education can safely treat with contempt and indifference whatever poison the rising generation may receive in churches, or from their parents, who are in many instances bigots, for the oil of a good education as an antidote is sufficient to remove all danger from the nation's life. And as to the assertion that Protestantism will perish, I reply only its errors will perish.

I have in several parts of the criticism omitted some of the thoughts of the most advanced thinkers on religion, for I would not intentionally hurt the feelings of any liberal Christians of sects that are by degrees

casting away the superstitions and cruel doctrines that have descended to
every church from the barbarous religions of former ages.   Such churches
and Christians should not be too severely criticised, but rather encouraged
in the cultivation and development of higher and nobler ideas of the
glorious attributes of an Almighty Creator by a more careful study of His
works and of the laws by which He governs on earth; but every lover of
progress should denounce and resist all those churches that have the
unreasonable audacity to declare that an All Wise Creator has given them
the power to become the spiritual dictators of the rest of mankind.

Our ministers should preach the gospel.
Spread far its glorious light;
But carry no sword in the other hand,
With which in battle to fight
Against the rude barbarians.
Who will not its truth receive,
'Tis against the Bible's precepts.
'Tis not alone their preaching
That will convert the human race.
For oft the best of preachers
Their calling do disgrace,
By not keeping the precepts,
Which they do the people teach.
'Tis by example, not by precept.
That the sinner's heart is reached,
Why should God's most holy servant.
Who believes in the truths of His word,
Owe debts unto his neighbor.
Then with him break his word
By not being able to pay on that date.
That which he promised his neighbor to pay,
And the kind hearted creditor
Does promise to wait.
How often do clergymen break their word
        in this way,
Till most of their parishoners,
With interest can listen no longer.

To the words of eloquence uttered by lips,
Which far from truth's paths wander.
Others must have their social pipe,
Or harmless glass of wine,
Others at a game of chess or draughts
Pass hours of their time,
Can this be done unto God's glory.
While souls are perishing each day
For the want of the gospel's blessed story?
Its bright, illuminating ray,
Has shone in most parts of the earth,
Where Christian influence is felt.
Though eighteen hundred years have passed
Since Christ on this earth dwelt.
Still ignorance and vice,
Upon this earth remain.
Men living in Christian land,
Take God's holy name in vain.
Alas! why should the scoffer
The opportunity have,
To mock at Christ's religion,
And at its failings laugh,
Point towards it with derision.
To the martyrs at the stake,
Burnt there by fellow Christians,
For some difference of faith.

— ◆◆◆ —

Our country is the greatest
That exists upon the earth,
And in modern civilization,
It truly ranks the first.
It has no monstrous serpents,
With which some lands are cursed,
No earthquakes burst upon us,
Nor famine's dreadful dearth
Has ever been throughout our land.
Since on its shores we have been;
No tyrant rules our noble land,
No deserts here are seen,
Our boundaries are the ocean's wave.
Our rivers broad and deep,
On which our ships can loaded sail
Till the ocean's waves they meet.
Our people are brought together
By railways of great length,
'Tis what our country was in need of
On account of its extent.
Now let us all as men and brothers.

In friendship meet together
And on every successive year,
Try and make our country better,
Let us give the hand of fellowship
Unto every man,
No matter what his creed or color,
As long as he is a man,
As long as he has honor,
And does himself respect,
Does keep our country's laws.
That man should justice get,
Cannot the foreign settlers.
The Saxon and the Celt.
The Protestants and Catholics
Their animosities forget,
Be a united nation,
Forget their ancient feuds.
Which cause naught but vexation
And the nation's honor lose;
Besides our being laughed at,
By the skeptics of this age,

That the followers of a Saviour meek,
Should against each other wage
In useless controversial strife,
Each other's creed condemn.
Is this being to the world a light?
Does this convert their fellowmen?
Ah, no; alas! it brings disgrace
Upon the Christian world.
Ignorance and vice there still remain,
In Christian lands abound,
Why try and pull the tiny mote
Out of our brother's eye,
When ten times worse in ours remain.
When thousands yearly die,
That hear the sound of our church's bells.
But die a fearful death,
Risking the woes of eternal hell,
By the sinful life they lead;
If we glance upon the surface,
Of our modern society.
There all things may appear
In accordance with propriety.
But go beneath the surface,
Until well amongst the people.
And inconsistencies are found,
From the college to the steeple,
Which disgrace this Christian nation.
Of this enlightened age,
And our progress does retard.
Towards the goal for which we aim.

Let our ministers and priests
Preach their doctrines side by side,
And not each others' creeds condemn.
God alone will this decide.
Let each religion and its followers
Banish their glaring faults.
And not their brothers anathemize,
Who through ignorance are at fault.
Let all our men and youth,
Throughout our territory,
Excel in honor's great pursuit.
With friendly rivalry;
Let the sturdy farmer with honest soil,
Turn the desert's dreary waste
Into a rich and fertile soil;
Bearing produce for the human race.
Let him ne'er be ashamed
Of his brawny arm,
His clothes or his sunburnt face.
But rather blush for an untilled farm,
Or a disorderly, ill kept place.
'Tis not fine nor gay apparel.
Or jewels of value great,
Though high may be his standing,
These will make no man great.
'Tis virtue and true ambition,
That enobles a man's heart;
If any man does lack these two.
With him does honor part.

Education is one of the grandest words ever uttered by mortal tongue. It elevates man from a position little better than that of the brute beast and makes him the most glorious creature on the face of the earth—on it depends the progress and civilization of the human race. Man can never attain to that exalted position for which he was created without the civilizing influence of a liberal education. Education in its highest and truest sense is the acquisition of moral, physical and scientific truths. It is according as nations and men become acquainted with these truths that they rise in the scale of modern civilization. But the majority of mankind of the present day do not receive education in its highest and truest sense, and for this reason millions of our fellow men can never attain to an exalted manhood through the ignorance, vice and superstition with which they are debased, and their degraded condition can only be attributed to the false and superficial education that they receive. Of the secular and religious education of the Mohammedans and pagans I have no need to speak, for the depravity and brutality of the majority of the believers in those religions is sufficient to show any civilized man of intelligence how a false religious education prevents man from becoming a civilized being. The great mistake in the religious instruction of the Christian churches is that too much precious time is wasted in teaching doctrines and creeds, which only create animosity and hatred between the nations of the earth. Some of these doctrines are an outrage on the justice and mercy of God and unworthy of the better feelings of humanity; for instance, there are Christian churches that have a doctrine in their prayer books stating that no one outside of Christianity can be saved, and this cruel and blasphemous doctrine is taught to millions of little innocent children. Those churches that teach doctrines contrary to science and humanity deserve the contempt of all civilized men. All men who take an interest in the

10

improvement of the human race should rebel against having their children taught such atrocious doctrines as these.

In some countries prayers and catechism is the only education the children receive.

In Lower Canada I have seen school examiners listen to a school teacher examining her scholars in the gravest manner possible and in most cases give a satisfactory report of their progress, yet, actually, these men could no more read or write in their native language than they could decipher the hieroglyphics on an ancient Egyptian tomb. To the priest who always attends these examinations it was a matter of indifference. He is generally satisfied if the scholars can repeat their prayers at a speed that would defy the most skillful phonographer to report them.

Could such an education as this make noble men and woman? It could not. History clearly shows us that religion amongst a people without education, and in consequence deprived of a proper use of their reasoning faculties, degenerates into superstitions and silly ceremonies, which are only remnants of ancient barbarity. Man must use his intellect and reason in religion as well as in everything else. God surely did not give man the grand intellect he possesses to use it merely in the earthly business of his life, or require him to accept with unquestioning belief doctrines that descend to him from his superstitious forefathers, or the many barbarous rites and ceremonies of his semi-civilized ancestors.

There are but few who do not admire the truths of Christianity, and these truths we ought to follow as far as they tend to improve and elevate the human race; but those churches that wish to retain any influence on the mind of man must keep up with the progress of civilization. Those that do not, and declare that theirs is a perfect church and keep its followers in spiritual slavery and have not the moral courage to do away with every ceremony and doctrine that are repulsive to the nobler sentiments of this more enlightened age, will lose their power and surely perish before the invincible light of truth—for that age is fast approaching in which error cannot be hid. Whether it is spiritual or temporal, it will be exposed to the pure and searching light of civilization and will be judged accordingly by every civilized and intelligent man.

Those churches that do not uphold the glorious principles of liberty and education, and whose churches are not surrounded with the evidences of the beneficial effects of their teachings, will be destroyed by the irresistible force of science and civilization. Though tyranny, ignorance and superstition are still ascendant on the earth, casting a gloom on some of its fairest portions, it will ere long be dispelled and vanish as the light of science and civilization spreads throughout the earth.

Let us not transmit to our descendants the religious error and superstition of our ancestors.

Let us use wisely the reasoning powers we possess for the advancement of truth and mankind, even though spiritual tyrants may threaten us with condemnation for doing so. Let us treat with scorn and contempt their impious threats and abuse and have our religion accord with science and reason, even though it may be called spiritual treason. And though some bigoted Christians may call it profanity, religion should not contradict science and humanity.

In the secular education of man the great mistake made is that the teaching of morals and the duties of life is almost wholly left to the instruction of religious teachers. This should not be permitted in any civilized country—for, by this system, some of the youth of the country receive no training at all from their worthless and ignorant parents, and others receive the prejudiced and narrow-minded instruction of sectarian schools, which is totally unsuited for the production of patriotic and liberal minded citizens.

The institutions of no nation are safe that gives perfect political and religious liberty to its citizens, and at the same time allows sects and denominations to give the inhabitants an education that is strictly antagonistic to the institutions of the country. Sectarian education and ignorance, are, without doubt, the deadliest enemies to all Republican forms of government. A Republican form of government is the truest and best, when the inhabitants are sufficiently enlightened to truly appreciate the great blessings of religious and political liberty. But for bigoted and ignorant people, it is the worst form of government imaginable, for the very reason that liberty is put to a base and dishonorable use. And even in highly civilized countries like the United States, this unlimited political and religious liberty is a source of danger to the institutions of the country on account of the treacherous and disloyal use that the Catholic church and some of its followers make of it. As in New York, for instance, where the ignorant foreign element has become so powerful that they may be considered the dominant party, and through their corrupt administration the civil government of New York is one of the most extravagant in America. Is not this a shameful state of affairs in the metropolis of the nation? A clear proof that it is the government's duty to Americanize and bring in harmony with the institution of the country all ignorant foreigners, by obliging them to receive a liberal education at national schools, and to disfranchise all those who through ignorance are unworthy to have a voice in the government of any civilized nation. Our government ought to awake to the reality of the responsibilities that devolve on it forming the character and sentiments of the rising generation of this country. Thousands of foreigners are yearly becoming citizens of this great republic. A great many of these, with many of the thousands already settled in the country, are giving their children an education that is making them narrow-minded, bigoted citizens. Many of whom through the pernicious influence of their education have only a half hearted loyalty to the institutions of this republic, and believe that they owe their first allegiance to their church and its spiritual ruler. If nothing is done to counteract this, and this class of citizens keep on increasing as they have done during the last half century, and our government admits a few more States with such ignorant people as the natives of New Mexico, the glorious institutions that our noble ancestors fought and died for, will be overthrown by the ignorant and prejudiced votes of the followers of a church that has already overthrown the institutions of Ancient Rome, Mexico, Peru and several other countries. All governments should adopt a national system of education. But for this Republic it is absolutely necessary to create universal peace, harmony and patriotism among its citizens, both native and foreign. All liberal and patriotic citizens of this republic should use their utmost endeavor to have a system of national schools established throughout every State of the Union with laws of compulsory attendance to those schools irrespective of religion or nationality, giving the youth of the country a good secular education and instruction in moral and nature's laws. This is all that is necessary to make good and useful citizens, and would counteract the pernicious effect of the prejudiced instruction that certain portions of American citizens receive at their homes and in their churches from their spiritual instructors. If the rising generation of this Republic receive an education like this during the next half century, the country's institutions will not be endangered by the Roman Catholic hierarchy or any other hierarchy. For the liberal national education will weaken the influence of the priesthood on the minds of the people, to such an extent as to render them and their doctrines harmless.

All men with a true interest in the progress of the human race should favor a system of universal, national education, that would teach man only the practical truths of life, which is required to make him a noble and sensible inhabitant of the world. Such an education as this would not make men infidels, although some religious frauds and impostors declare that it would. It would not make men deny the existence of God, but would give them a higher and grander idea of His glorious majesty, and cast forever from the soul of man the shackles of spiritual slavery. To the want of this system of education, may be attributed most of the evils of society of the present day. Though education in this country has wrought a great and glorious work there still remains a great deal to accomplish; though schools and colleges are built throughout the land, ignorance has not disappeared. Thousands in ignorance still remain a disgrace to the age we live in, because ignorant parents are unable to instill into the minds of their children a worthy ambition to elevate themselves to that honorable position that the civilizing influence of education generally enables its lover to attain. And there are millions in a condition little better than that of ignorance; though they have gone to school and learned to read and write, they can only do so in a most indifferent manner; though they have the use of speech and sound intelligent brains, they cannot express their sentiments and ideas, in a clear and proper manner. Yet these people spend hours of precious time in senseless chat and silly games, and then falsely say, they have no time to educate themselves. There is not a man living, that cannot find time to give himself a good elementary education; even by studying only one hour a day, it can be accomplished. But, strange to say, this portion of mankind seem to be of the opinion that man's recreation must be of a frivolous and useless sort, such as silly, childish games and conversation. Why should it? Surely man after physical exertion could just as well find physical rest, by taking advantage of the glorious opportunities that this age affords them, an age of cheap literature, clever authors and excellent newspapers, which are all capable of imparting both knowledge and pleasure at the same time. It must justly be acknowledged that all men who disregard these advantages deserve the contemptible position they occupy in society of the present day, and have no reason to complain, if society refuses to tolerate them in its midst. For every man by self-culture can fit himself for the society of the best educated men and women of the present age. This to some may appear an exaggerated view of the question, but those who think so should bear in mind that a man need not be a Greek scholar or mathematician, to receive a welcome in the best of society. Any man who can grammatically and intelligently express his opinion on the leading topics of the day, can enjoy the society of the best men and women, no matter what his wealth or position may be. Of course he is looked down on by the giddy masculine and feminine butterflies of fashion, but the opinion of such creatures as these does not deserve a moment's consideration, for that day is fast approaching when the intellectual beauty of the human mind, will be a better passport into society, than costly dress or the possession of wealth. Even in the society of the present day, which almost worships the "almighty dollar," what a miserable and contemptible position does the vulgar wealthy man occupy! he is merely tolerated by a certain class of good society. And to him is lost forever, one of the greatest pleasures of man on earth, that is the true enjoyment of the society of the best and most refined of mankind. If, however, the noble sons of toil deserve criticism for their want of self-culture, no words can express the contempt, that many of the members of the best society deserve for the idle, worthless lives they lead. For much to the honor of the sons of toil, and to the shame of the upper classes, the lower class of society has produced nearly as many great men as the upper class, and some of them have been the brightest ornaments of society. But what better can be expected when thousands of ladies and gentlemen think because they have an excellent education, elegant manners and great wealth that they can consider themselves exempt from all the labor and cares, physical and mental, of this life. On the contrary their greater advantages should inspire them with an exalted desire to acomplish much for the honor and advancement of themselves and the age they live in. A contrary idea, however, seems to be entertained by thousands of the members of the upper classes of the present day; the consequence is thousands of ladies and gentlemen with talents, wealth and education waste their valuable lives without accomplishing anything great, or good for themselves, or the age they live in. They may have been honest and virtuous men and women, and dressed in broadcloth and silk, wore diamond rings, kept many servants, kept a well furnished table and enjoyed life with their friends, but what of that? To them this was no credit; they only spent what their fathers earned, although they did not exceed their income, they did not increase it. If all mankind were to act thus, civilization's progress would cease and man would become a stagnant and ignoble creature. It must not be imagined however, that these lazy, luxurious and worthless inhabitants of the world, enjoy the highest degree of happiness. For the highest, purest and greatest happiness, can only be obtained by great and noble actions. It is the duty of good society to use its influence for the improvement, elevation and developement of the human race. For its influence is one of the greatest, most powerful and best means of educating man. But alas! even some of the best circles of society, forget their own and the country's honor; smile on men who are utterly destitute of most of the noble attributes that man should possess, and for this reason the circles of some of the best of society, are disgraced with thousands of ladies and gentlemen, who pass through life in a careless, sluggish way, a living disgrace to society and themselves. There are also thousands of wealthy ladies, that waste their lives in doing nothing else than going to places of amusement, and in useless conversation in their drawing rooms. They do not even take care of their children; and in many cases the only useful work they do is a little ornamental crotchet. I would not intentionally say one word to hurt the feelings of any lady, for we all owe them a debt of gratitude, for elegance, beauty and comfort of our homes, and for the elevating and ennobling influence they exercise on us as mothers, wives and sisters. But it must be acknowledged that ladies with the opportunities I have just mentioned, should have higher, nobler aspirations than to be merely a leader of fashions and a maker of anti-macassers. Could they not more honorably employ their time in perfecting their intellectual development, for there is nothing to prevent such ladies as these being bright lights in the literary and scientific world. It is no use for them to say "society does not expect this of us, it is satisfied if we merely remain as ornamental dolls in our drawing rooms." If society did and does entertain this barbarous view of the question, there can be no doubt that it is quickly disappearing before the wiser and more civilized view that women ought and can be man's equal in intellectual pursuits, if she properly cultivates her intellectual powers and that the physical and mental development of the human race is dependent upon physical and mental improvement of both sexes. Should not good society that takes an interest in man's improvement make such ladies ashamed of their idle and useless lives, by refusing to tolerate them in its midst, and should not ladies that take a true interest in civilization refuse to acknowledge as friends all gentlemen who live worthless lives, no matter how polished they are or how well they may be received in that class of society who only regard a man's wealth and outer polish. Society ought to have an honorable ambition to increase the nobility of man by encouraging every virtue that adds physical and mental strength and beauty to the human race, and discourage all habits, customs and fashions, whether of dress or diet, or otherwise, that are detrimental to man's physical and mental development. Until society does this, the world will never fully realize the grand meaning of the word, or what an exalted and noble being man can become.

LIFE'S REAL ROMANCE;

A PICTURE FROM LIFE FROM 1838 TO 1883.

Volume 1 for sale at the leading book stores in Salt Lake City, at Harper Bros.'
Franklin Square Library, New York, and at W. Drysdales & Co., 23. St. James Street,
Montreal.
The Second Volume will be ready for sale by the first of November.

CONTENTS OF VOLUME SECOND.

education; home life amongst the French; an Irish-Canadian wake and funeral; the noble sentiments of an association of young men; how young Frenchmen court their sweethearts; amusing incidents among the French inhabitants.

CHAPTER V.—Quebec politics; an extraordinary long letter, full of spiritual and temporal advice; a Canadian champion; a picture of a party given by English settlers; my first attendence at midnight mass; a silent conflict between right and wrong; a wolf in sheep's clothing; boyish love; French festivities before Lent; some of the inconsistencies of the Christian churches discussed,

CHAPTER VI.—A French wedding described; in English districts; Traveling under difficulties; a second Vicar of Wakefield; first experience of farming on a cleared farm; a sugar party; good resolutions; a people devoid of the delicate sensibility of civilized men; the prayer of a young man religiously inclined; my first attempts at poetry; a conversation with two Parisian socialists; my opinions on predestination; farming under difficulties; the two wildest young ladies I ever met; a wealthy, vulgar, Bombastic family; a gloomy Englishman's letter; wise advise against the credit system; a discussion of Irish affairs with an Irishman.

CHAPTER VII.—My beau ideal of feminine grace and beauty; the errors of Romanism exposed; a prayer, to which even Infidels would not object; a discussion between a high and low churchman; a country rustic among city ladies; how Canadian school teachers are treated; a Liberal's opinion on provincial politics; sentimental verses; an ambitious young man.

CHAPTER VIII.—A delightful evening party; the condition of farmers as a class discussed; some of the faults of French soldiers; Canadian winter sports; how young people enjoy a church decoration; rather rough Frenchmen; many adverse and favorable opinions on army life; the Bible as a rule of faith; contemptuous sarcastic letters; how the two lovers were parted; a sentimertal young man in yonng ladies' society.

CHAPTER IX.—An evening with vulgar English girls; a young man ashamed of his grandmother; a spoiled son; an evening's conversation of a French family almost taken down verbatim; a rustic's opinion of etiquette;

CHAPTER X.—The course of study of English army officers compared with that of the United States; six letters of General Washington to an Irish friend of the American revolutionists; Canadian scenery described; condensed news of the day; valuable statistics.

CONTENTS OF VOLUME THIRD.

CHAPTER I.—Three years' correspondence between two Canadian farmers, containing much interesting and useful information of life on a farm; an eastern farmer's opinion of the great northwest; a village genius, criticisms on Canadian society; fragmentary verses on morality and religion.

CHAPTER II.—A poem of 50 verses, describing from history the condition of the English people in the age of chivalry; a devoted admirer of music; how fair ladies encourage antagonisim amongst their admirers, amateur theatricals amongst country people; a poem revealing the darkest side of human nature; how I lost a grand opportunity; Canadian villages behind the age.

CHAPTER III.—Socialistic pugilistic laborers; a criticism on the churches of England; a red hot argument between a Catholic and a Protestant; sentimental verses; an evening spent with an upstart family; how the French-Canadians conduct themselves at a picnic; pugilistic young ladies; a trip through the finest agricultural district of Canada; a flowery French-Canadian orator: how some of the Catholic churches are built in Canada; a district of drunkards; melancholy meditations of a love sick young man; a model lady guest.

CHAPTER IV.—The terrific grandeur of forest fires: a Canadian exhibition at Montreal minutely described; a 60 verse poem describing early settlers' lives and difficulties in the Canadian backwoods; conflicting opinions on theater going: an inconoclastic letter; the trials of a drunkard's wife; the terrible death of a drunkard and opium eater; how much good a faithful Christian can accomplish; the letter of an ignoramus; a season of gaiety at the theaters, concerts, church bazars, socials and parties; a bitter denunciation of vulgarity; forcible arguments against fictitious supernatural religion.

CHAPTER IX.—Everyday life amongst Canadian lumbermen; how war might be suppressed; conflicting opinions for and against the Pope's temporal power; how farmers are ruined by the credit system; a very severe literary critic; a prejudiced view of the "far west"; an Irish land question ably discussed; a condensed history of Canada's greatest, city with interesting statistics; a religious, gentle, loving cousin; rather harsh opinions on Canadian farmers; noble resolutions of a young man; correspondence on war with many conflicting ideas on it; correspondence on education; evenings at cards, rides, drives, parties, dancing, croquet, picnics and conversations; Jewishism exposed as an enemy to civilization; Catholic and Protestant persecutions compared; love's ennobling influence; the scandals of a French village; English influence on the French-Canadians; a model letter of condolence; a quarrelsome husband and wife; old and new system of making maple sugar; death scene in a French-Canadian house.

CHAPTER X.—A few specimens of terrible French oaths; the city and the country around Quebec described; an able defence of Roman Catholicism; selected letters from Irish correspondents containing much of interest about that country; England's policy in Ireland severely criticised; the opinions of Irishmen in Canada on Irish affairs: geology's contradiction of sacred history; resolutions of a pious young man; nature's noblemen and superficially polished gentlemen compared; disagreeable letters; an unpleasant state of affairs; a Frenchman's grievances against his wife and his barbarous idea of his duty towards his children: some incidents exhibiting the lamentable depravity of man; how an old maid was insulted; how English Protestants manage their church affairs in parts of Canada; verses containing a forcible condemnation of the despicable habit of quizzing; verses on childhood; various models of feminine loveliness described; thirty verses describing the advantages of an Irishman in America; a picnic amongst low, vulgar English settlers; selected English correspondence containing much of interest about England; French-Canadians and their lives criticised; the pernicious effect of vulgar associations; abandonment of farming; a miserable college; a drunken French family; a sketch of different queer looking specimens of humanity, as seen in a country ball room; how the Italian musicians were insulted; a perfectly impartial view of the land question in Great Britian; in a drunken row amongst the French; an audacious young rascal's robbery; my last letter to a benefactor; farewell to old friends; Canadian scenery; condensed news and great events of the day; valuable statistics.

CONTENTS OF VOLUME FOURTH.

www.ingramcontent.com/pod-product-compliance
Lightning Source LLC
Chambersburg PA
CBHW020729100426
42735CB00038B/1407